D1166363

EAS Syndrome

Healing Burnout In Adults
Lacking Parental Affirmation

Trevor Walters

With Jim Stanley, M.D.

Anglican House

Second Printing October 2016

Published by Anglican House Media Ministry, Inc., Newport Beach, California. You may contact us at *anglicanhousemedia.org* Text set in Optima typeface. Printed by Asia Printing Co., Ltd., Seoul, Korea.

ANGLICAN HOUSE
MEDIA MINISTRY

ISBN: 978-0-9970167-0-3

Endorsements

David Stoop   Psychologist and Co-Host of the Nationally Syndicated Radio & TV Program, *New Life Live*

"For Pastors and other Christian Leaders, burnout is almost an epidemic, and it often leads to the end of a ministry. How refreshing to be shown so clearly that the problem of burnout is not the result of what we typically blame, the stress of the job. Instead, the issue revolves around the relationship we have with our earthly fathers.

"In the Old Testament, fathers blessed their children as a way of launching them into adulthood. Today, we don't usually call it "the blessing." However, it is still what we long to receive from our father – his approval of who we are. But for generations, that approval from Dad has been missing for both sons and daughters, mainly because it was missing in our father's life as well.

"Trevor Walters not only shows us 'why' this is true, he also shows us 'how' the healing process can be experienced. Instead of burning out due to an approval deficit, and experiencing its consequences, we can and must learn to satisfy that painful deficit so that we can ultimately 'finish well.' "

J.I Packer   Eminent Theologian and Prolific Author

"Bishop Walters writes from long counseling ministry and in weighty professional partnership about how lack of parental affirmation in one's growing years induces midlife burnout and breakdown, and faith in Christ brings resources for rebuilding. This is a masterly book that will enrich all therapeutic counselors, Christians especially."

Jack Balswick   Senior Professor, Sociology & Family Development, Fuller Theological Seminary

"I wish this book had been available when I was teaching my seminary course in human development – it is spot on, both in identifying why persons in ministry often experience career burnout, and in pointing towards the path of healing and recovery. I strongly recommend this book for persons preparing for ministry or preparing others for ministry."

Philip Ashey   Chief Executive Officer, American Anglican Council

"I have had the privilege of lecturing and ministering to Anglican clergy with Bishop Trevor Walters, and can attest to the power of his insights into the causes for burnout among clergy and other caring professionals. It is not only his understanding of the causes, but his sound suggestions of how we can find healing, recovery, and fresh strength in Christ to move beyond burnout that clergy and others have found so helpful. At a time when record numbers of clergy are leaving the ministry monthly due to burnout and moral failure, this book is a timely prescription for leaders who want to start and finish well, and in Christ!"

Michael Nazir-Ali   Eminent Church of England Cleric. President, Oxford Centre for Training, Research, Advocacy & Dialogue

"This is a timely book. Just as fathers are being written out of law and society, the research is showing, more and more, their importance for a child's development, relationships with peers and the ability to form healthy friendships across gender and generational divides. Bishop Trevor shows how a deficit in this relationship can cause a lack of balance in our approach to life and work. He then set out an authentically Christian way of dealing with the past so that the present may be healed and so that the future is productive for the Gospel."

Author's Note

Here is my *own confession as a recovering External Affirmation* Syndrome (EAS) sufferer. When I was 35 years old and living in Calgary I found myself clipping an article out of the *Calgary Herald* newspaper. It was about the role I had played in starting up a Telephone Distress Line.

My wife Julie called out to me from the kitchen, "What are you doing?" I was caught red-handed in the act of "clipping."

"Nothing," I mumbled.

She pressed. "*What are* you doing?"

"Oh, just sending an article to the UK."

She nailed me, very deftly.

"Still trying to get your Dad's approval?"

"Ah . . . No."

We both knew it was a lame answer.

But it was my turning point. From that moment on denial gave way to admission that even at 35 I was in the grip of needing to have my father's affirmation.

This book was called into being from the moment Julie *insisted, "What are* you . . ."* I had intended to write it some 30 years ago, because my own recovery from EAS was so liberating. But I was busy and enjoying my release. I suppose I hadn't really wanted to look back. That is until recently when sharing some of this material with a colleague made me realize I could point others to a way out of an awful imprisonment.

Dedication

This book is dedicated to my children Sarah, Mark and Tim who, sadly, suffered from not getting sufficient affirmation from me. Yet they love me despite my failings as a parent. My actions were inexcusable, and I have had to ask their forgiveness, and our Heavenly Father's. I am so grateful for their gracious forgiveness. I am very, very proud of each of them and love them dearly!

Trevor Walters

Contents

Contents

1

What this Book is About

This book is about what my experience leads me to believe is the usual cause of *midlife burnout* (i.e., mental and emotional exhaustion) in professionals and other high-functioning people, both men and women.

Usual cause?

Really? How can you say that?

Because in counseling hundreds of burned-out clergy I have confirmed that the usual cause of their hitting the wall is the failure of their earthly father to have truly given them his blessing. So they devote their lives to seeking affirmation elsewhere, a very taxing endeavor they can sustain only so long before finally burning-out in midlife. And because pastoring ranks among the very most stressful occupations in North America,[1] I think my finding is equally applicable to burnout of people in other high stress occupations.

---

[1] For example, pastors are at far greater risk for depression than individuals with other occupations, an ongoing study by the Clergy Health Initiative at Duke Divinity School has found. The research is part of a study conducted in 2008, 2010, 2012 and 2014 that is scheduled to continue into 2016. *www.clergyhealthinitiative.org.*

More exactly this book is about a way out of External Affirmation Syndrome's horrible jailhouse.

Before proceeding I need to acknowledge that there are a number of very good books about the benefits – indeed the *necessity* – of a father's or parents' blessing in the lives of children. I list some in Appendix 2 and acknowledge there may be others I've missed and that should have been included. But, as far as I'm aware, until now, no book has related the absence of a father's blessing to burnout in high-functioning individuals.

Okay, Let's Get Started

At this point you may be saying, "Well okay but this doesn't apply to me. My father and I have lunch or supper almost weekly. Maybe this describes my sister a little, but not me."

Ah, but there's a central truth you need to get straight in your head: rebellion and compliance share the same mainspring. Both are reactions to an authority figure. Rebellion acts-out while compliance "acts in." One child decides they'll never get approval and moves off somewhere. Another child thinks, "If I'm really, truly successful, Dad will eventually come around to me." Sadly, the words of affirmation almost never come! The child grows and ages but never hears, "You are my beloved son (or daughter) in whom I am well pleased."

You figured out long ago your father and you were oil and water – you just didn't go together. Maybe you've put lots of real estate between you. Or maybe with a sigh of relief you left home as soon as you could. However, if you are a godly person you've a lingering problem. Certainly you do if you're a Christian. You *must* forgive him!

Well, you say, you've done that. You've gone ahead and "forgiven him." So how is it that you still bristle when you're around him? Or something can twinge in your gut when you think of him? (More on forgiveness a little later)

Here's another thing to firmly grasp as we're getting started. The primary source of affirmation in childhood may transfer to a brother, teacher, priest or other person when the father is absent or passive. When parents are weak, or absent, one's need for affirmation doesn't just atrophy like an unused muscle. No, the opposite is true. The need for approval takes on an even greater importance in your life. And your quest for affirmation *migrates* from your father or parents to other people – to brothers or sisters, teachers, employers, your superiors, or religious leaders. Other people now hold in their hands a powerful influence in your life and, like parental figures, they too can upset your equilibrium when they too fail to affirm you.

Here We Go

First of all this book grounds blessing and affirmation in sound Biblical theology, and from my nearly 40 years of pastoral counseling in this field. It contains –

• A process to heal the *wound* of not having received your father's (or parents') blessing,

- Results of case studies to illustrate the curse of affirmation withheld and the joy of deliverance from its consequences, and

- A definite roadmap to living vibrantly and productively without your earthly parent's blessing.

At the center of this therapy is an important metaphor, the *Cup*. One's "cup" represents their repository for approval and affirmation; one's cup needs to be filled and remain so.

Parents are called by God to fill up a child's cup with words and acts that affirm. But just as children who are not fed enough food may go into the streets to beg, a person who doesn't receive enough affirmation will go "into the streets" seeking it. We see this as habitually offering your cup to be filled, and we call it External Affirmation Syndrome or *EAS*.

The Chronic Need

A man or woman having been blessed and affirmed by their father or parents will put their cup away between meals. This is not so among EAS sufferers. They have a chronic or frequent need for affirmation. The need is so great that they carry their cup around in life begging for any morsel of affirmation.

At this point you may be thinking, "This isn't me. I would never do that."

Ah, so now we come to the pivot point of this book.

4

The insidious thing about EAS is that its sufferers are unaware that chronically seeking affirmation is pulling them along a path to a midlife burnout.

Nor are EAS sufferers discriminating in what they will accept into their cup. Unaware of their vulnerability, they can't protect their cup when in the presence of people whose neglect or hurtful words may penetrate deeply. Damage inflicted by parents or other authority figures can jostle the metaphoric cup causing spillage or, worse still, puncture the cup. And then when the child or grownup does get some real affirmation from their "begging" it can drain from their cup with little or no benefit gained. Then the sufferer dismisses it by internalizing, "Well, my parents who really knew me couldn't see my worth, so this guy is probably saying it just to be nice . . . probably even says this to everyone."

So What's the Answer?

First of all, to show someone a way out before they agree they're actually caught-up in a serious problem is rather like casting pearls before swine. Nothing wrong with swine of course; they just don't see a benefit in pearls.

And fear not, I won't be offering quick-fix counsel, like the seven steps to this or ten steps to the other thing. Not even "you have to forgive them and move on in life" or even "just let Jesus fill your cup."

Gratuitous advice could and should cause you to ditch this book, pronto! Indeed if someone had said something like that to me at an earlier stage in my life I would have dismissed it with a hearty *"been there, done that!"*

You've likely already said several varieties of confessions regarding your parents but whatever the secret of success it doesn't appear to be in the wording, does it? Does an urge to forgive somehow keep on reasserting itself? What's the secret here? Is there one? Or are you the unforgivable one where repentance fails to bring peace?

Truth be told both forgiveness and Jesus filling your cup are indeed at the heart of my methodology. Trust me, though. For your sake getting to it becomes a question of timing.

Logic and Feelings

Finally in this introductory chapter I want to focus on your feelings and your imagination.

What, you say?

All right, I'll admit it! I am attempting to soften you up to trust feelings and your imagination as a place where God speaks – but *neither more nor less* than how he speaks through your mind and logic.

For example, we see in the Psalms a people who let reason and feelings flow into each other. There is no hierarchy there, no tension between feelings and logic. Reason does not scold feelings for being the distrusted evil, second cousin, once removed. No, for the Psalmist the two truths coexisted. Objective truth and subjective truth were two sides of a coin, both of them requiring recognition.[2]

Now here comes the thing I want you to see clearly. When the going gets tough and circumstances sorely challenge one's faith, we can have seasons of not having feelings. Even faith itself can come under siege and disappear for a season. But the Christian life depends on the facts of the Christian Faith, and even when one's subjective evaluation fails it doesn't destroy Christianity. When I am not feeling God it doesn't diminish God one iota.

Feelings are very important, and to remain bereft of them is certainly unhealthy. Consider a marriage. How long can an intimate relationship last if feelings go missing? I would suggest that one's relationship with God is rather like a marriage. Perhaps your own relationships, including the one with your Heavenly Father, have been going sour precisely because you have not been able to keep your feelings on track. I'll suggest further that we need to employ reason here too, employ it for the purpose of rescuing feeling.

---

[2] Indeed Evangelical Christian thought may be coming to this understanding, having moved significantly over the last 20 years toward affirming the validity and importance of emotion in the Christian life. Emerging as they did in the early 19th Century at the height of the scientific revolution (where mind over emotion was the order of the day) Evangelicals had embellished Aquinas's view that reason is superior to emotion, as for them memory of a former culture, Judaism, with its passionate Psalms, had faded.

I believe that by thinking through logically the many aspects of childhood, and reasoning out what is the truth concerning memories, you can release your emotions that have been held captive by untruths.

Let me illustrate. When I was a University Chaplain in Calgary I had the privilege of ministering to one of the scientists. He came to me with the issue of "not feeling the presence of God in my life." He took a scientific approach to his faith, seeking to test exhaustively the theory that if he prayed and read scripture daily God would reveal himself. This was a patient and faithful man, but in his case twenty-four years of such devotion with no gift of the presence was too long a wait for even the most seasoned of researchers.

His feelings had crashed and burned in childhood many years before, but he had continued on as if everything was perfectly normal. A man without feelings! But over our six-month journey together he came to trust his feelings and to "give back" to his parents their harsh treatment of him. Not only did he experience the warm, loving presence of Jesus as a living friend, his wife reported that he had become quite warm, open, and expressive in their relationship. She was overjoyed as you can imagine after so long a wait on her part.

It is deeply humbling to receive kind letters about transformation in people's lives and to meet up with them even years after the counseling described in this book. I want therefore to keep on extending the circle of those who find release from EAS. First, by sharing these tools with counselors who are looking for more tools for their toolbox. Secondly, I know that even without having access to a counselor this therapy will work for many people via the series of thought provoking exercises contained in this book, whereby they can regain control of their "affirmation cup" and learn to put it away between meals.

A Psychiatrist's Take

When pastoral counselors talk of diagnosis and treatment of emotional symptoms then the question comes up, "How does this relate to current thinking in the field of psychiatry?" The short answer is that the author's concepts and techniques are compatible in my opinion with mainstream practice of the American Psychiatric Association, with some minor exceptions.

The American Psychiatric Association (APA) lists all of its diagnoses in the 947 page *Diagnostic and Statistical Manual of Mental Disorders*, Fifth Edition (2013) or the DSM-V it is called. The author's proposed diagnosis of External Affirmation Syndrome is not in the DSM-V but that fact does not imply an incompatibility.

The DSM-V is a list of what are called mental disorders using the following definition: "A mental disorder is a syndrome characterized by clinically significant disturbance in an individual's cognition, emotion, regulation, or behavior that reflects a dysfunction in the psychological, biological, or developmental processes underlying mental functioning. Mental disorders are usually associated with significant distress or disability in social, occupational, or other important activities . . . This definition of mental disorder was developed for clinical, public health and research purposes." (p. 20).

The mental disorders in DSM-V are virtually all defined by published research data from multiple academic institutions and based on clients who have been treated in medical settings. So when our well trained, highly experienced pastoral counselor/author sees a definite pattern of symptoms in a number of his cases and finds it useful to put a label on it for his colleagues and his clients, then I believe it is a significant contribution. Incidentally, that is how many of the diagnoses in DSM-V got their start. Our author is not asking to have the External Affirmation Syndrome added to the DSM, but who knows what time and experience will bring.

Regarding the techniques for helping his clients, all of his procedures, in my opinion, are compatible with current psychiatric treatment. In the preface of DSM-V its authors state: "DSM has been used by clinicians and researchers from several different orientations (including biological, interpersonal, psychodynamic, cognitive behavioral, family/systems) all of whom strive for a common language to communicate the essential characteristics of the mental disorders presented by their patients." The treatment orientation of the author fits the definition above except for the biological. His techniques are widely accepted and are not practices that we should be skeptical about. A clear issue that distinguishes this book from secular academic psychiatry is the theological component – the author grounds the issue of blessings and affirmation in theology. This means that he and his clients believe in the divine healing power of Jesus. Before the counseling described here can begin the counselor and client must agree on this issue; but otherwise the process presented in this book is consistent with mainstream psychiatry.

Jim Stanley, M.D.

Trevor Walters

2

EAS Leads to Burnout

For more than 17 years now I have lectured and ministered at a retreat called Oasis. Six or seven times a year we have held weeklong retreats for pastors and missionaries who simply crashed and burned. These are residential retreats affording the beset attendees a safe and intimate opportunity for opi,lening up and sharing freely. From observation and dialogue, and from follow-up counseling with dozens of attendees over the years, I have been able to draw some supportable conclusions as to the usual cause of burnout in high-functioning professional people.

One might think as I had previously thought that what causes burnout in the lives of people in high stress jobs is too much of it over too many years; in other words, enduring excessive stress to the point they can't handle it anymore. I am no longer persuaded that such is always the case or that it is even usually the case.

Think about it. Many professionals who have vast amounts of stress knocking at their door day after day (e.g., trauma surgeons, trial lawyers, air traffic controllers) often describe their tasks as challenging and rewarding or even inspiring. Politicians are constantly at risk of making people unhappy and even furious with their decisions. Even when vilified in the media or mocked in the court of public opinion most politicians have the inner strength to cope and continue. In the imagery of President Harry S. Truman they can stand the heat in the kitchen.

My experience persuades me that burnout is caused not by outer pressure but by inner conflict which, when left untreated, eventually erodes the requisite inner fortitude. If outer conflict were the main cause of burnout then trial lawyers would surely top the list but they do not. Dentistry tops the list of professions with the highest rates of burnout. The practice of dentistry doesn't generate unrelenting stress. No angry conferences in the office, seldom an argument with a client or the lab. Nor are dentists as a class near the top of the list for chronic financial worries. No. We are left looking at inner conflict as the usual cause of burnout among dentists.

This book deals in the main with identifying and treating the usual source of an inner conflict that is strong and persistent enough to ignite midlife burnout in professional men and women. My years with Oasis and my counseling practice have led me to conclude that in most cases the operative inner conflict causing midlife burnout is *affirmation deficiency*. When parents fail in their task of affirming a son or daughter, the person embarks on a life long make-up quest to seek affirmation elsewhere. The cost of this quest in terms of quality of life is overwork, undue perfectionism, and anxieties, to name but few of the harmful consequences. This quest is a pursuit they can maintain only so long before burning out at around age 50. I call the condition External Affirmation Syndrome (EAS).

What do we mean by burnout? What are its symptoms? Without dwelling too much on the condition itself let us pause for a good look at burnout before getting on with our knowledge of EAS and, most importantly, an understanding of the means of releasing sufferers from its jaws. The following observations are from my counseling experience. While there is no statement that is universally accepted, I think most practitioners would tend to generally agree with the following points.

Observable Symptoms of Burnout

STAGE 1

- Insomnia / Broken sleep patterns
- Weakened immune system
- Restlessness / Loss of peace
- Loss of a vision / Disappointed in life
- Not participating in daily activities that used to delight / Loss of joy
- Fatigue
- Irritability / Fruits of the Spirit diminishing
- Frustration
- Inward criticism expressed as negative self talk
- Difficulty concentrating

15

- Running on adrenaline
- Swearing under breath
- Diminished impulse control
- Anxiety
- Seeking comfort in destructive ways: over-eating, pornography, fantasy, etc.
- Defensiveness
- Difficulty trusting other people
- Confusion
- Conflicted
- Avoidance / Putting off dealing with issues
- Digestive tract disturbances / Stomach problems
- Everything depends on me / I carry the weight of the world
- Feeling useless

STAGE 2

- Anger outbursts or anger at self
- Looking for or dreaming of another position as a way out.
- Critical of others
- Feeling hurt, let down, neglected, even overlooked by God
- Complaining

- Insomnia making daily functioning more difficult
- Bursts of adrenalin followed by crashes
- Changed work habits / Overworking and or working less efficiently
- Memory lapses, e.g., losing keys, forgetting previously known details
- Exhausted / Worn out
- Depressed
- Heart hardening towards God

STAGE 3

- Acute fear with likelihood of panic attacks
- Social phobia
- Paranoia
- Isolation
- Alienation of friends and allies
- Acute sensitivity to stimuli; i.e., sounds, sights, touch, smell
- Drastic reduction in physical ability and stamina
- Heart hardened towards God and others
- Too exhausted to be angry
- Spouse increasingly the brunt of the anger
- Easily moved to tears
- Acceptance of the need for extended time off.

In my opinion, the presence of 50% or more of these observable symptoms is suspicious for a diagnosis of burnout. It should be noted that this inventory overlaps a diagnosis of depression or post-traumatic stress disorder (PTSD). If a person also checks off more than 50% of the Affirmation Inventory at pages 74-75, then treatment of burnout caused by EAS is preferred.

3

A Father's Blessing

The difference between receiving a gift of his father's blessing – versus having earned it – wasn't lost on my 18 year-old. After a particularly outstanding report card, when I had praised him at length, he said something like this to me,

> *"You're always happy about what I've done, but I don't think you enjoy me for being . . . just me!"*

As painful as it was for me to hear, my son was right.

Sadly, my own education as a parent came too late to make the difference that I had wanted for my children. I had wanted so badly to give affirmation, unlike my own father who failed to offer much at all. And now as a parent I had rendered up such a poor facsimile of the real thing. I had to ask my son's, and my Heavenly Father's, forgiveness.

The Heavenly Template

A template is a pattern or guide used in making something accurately. With that in mind, let's have a look at the best example of fatherhood there is – God the Father. Pay attention now and keep this ever in mind: Jesus received his Father's blessing *before* he embarked on his ministry, not afterward. We read in Matthew's Gospel that "when Jesus was baptized, immediately he went up from the water, and behold, the heavens were opened to him, and he saw the Spirit of God descending like a dove and coming to rest on him; and behold, a voice from heaven said, 'This is my beloved Son, with whom I am well pleased.'" (Matthew 3:16,17)

His Father's blessing had enveloped Jesus before he could ever have done anything to earn it. He hadn't restored sight to the blind, healed the lame, restored hearing to th1e deaf, let alone raised the dead! And his Father's blessing was totally *grace*-based. It wasn't in the least dependent on any past achievement or any expectation of future performance. The Father's blessing – carrying such power into Jesus' earthly ministry – wasn't works-based in any sense at all, but what it did was to fill Jesus to overflowing with affirmation.

Maybe you're thinking, "Yes, but Jesus was divine, so this is well and good but what's it got to do with me, being a mere mortal?" If you think that then you are forgetting or missing a fundamental fact of the Christian faith, as stated in the Nicene Creed:

> "For us and for our salvation he came down from   heaven, was incarnate from the Holy Spirit and the Virgin Mary, and was made man."

Jesus Christ was and is all God and all man! There is no question about Jesus' need of his Father's blessing for the work to be done on earth; he would be tempted in his ministry just as we are (Hebrews 2:1; 4:15). Nor is there

20

any question about this: Jesus set the bar high but he didn't go around modeling behaviors that would be beyond our reach. His were behaviors we can adopt as our own, with God's help.[3]

Jesus took this precious filling – *knowing* that he was loved and enjoyed by the Father – into his trial by fire in the wilderness, and the Father's affirmation was always with him to sustain him through times of loneliness, shame, rejection, abandonment, and terminal abuse.

The blessing of his Father set Jesus free from the question: Am I loveable? Our earthly father's blessing can do the same for us. Once we have it, the quest for blessing is over and the fundamental developmental issue of identity is settled. My inner eyes are taken away from looking at myself; they are now *outwardly* focused, and I am released from the nagging questions of how I am presenting myself and what others may be thinking about me. I am now ready for the outer world of conflict, challenge, and even rejection. Maybe I'm even ready to seek out a new kind of fitting-in with others, like Dietrich Bonhoeffer's insight of the "life together" as it could and should be. I am set free to be attentive to Martin Buber's clear sense of intimacy – that love is the responsibility of

---

[3] This is well stated in the *collect* (corporate prayer) for the Second Sunday After Easter in the Anglican *Book of Common Prayer*: "ALMIGHTY God, who hast given thine only Son to be unto us both a sacrifice for sin, and also an ensample of godly life; Give us grace that we may always most thankfully receive that his inestimable benefit, and also daily endeavor ourselves to follow the blessed steps of his most holy life; through the same thy Son Jesus Christ our Lord. Amen."

an "I" for a "They." I can take my place on the team, as I do not need the team to take care of my identity and issues of worth. I am freed to be of service to others without needing or wanting to be paid in brownie points.

Jesus' Temptations – Relevant?

Let's have a look at Jesus' temptations. What if they afflict EAS victims too? They do, as I think you'll come to agree. Let's see how Jesus was empowered to engage the Devil by deflecting provocation and not internalizing it.

First the Devil mockingly questions Jesus' identity and his worth (Luke 4:3). He questions Jesus' identity with a taunt: "If you are the Son of God?" Then he proceeds to try to get Jesus to prove his relationship with his Father by doing something really special, like turning rocks into bread. Jesus had nothing to prove by good work. He knew he was a loved Son who already had his Father's affirmation. Jesus didn't bite – because his affirmation cup was full. So the first temptation fell flat.

It is easy to spot the analogous temptation plaguing EAS sufferers because the first temptation they'll fall for is working hard at trying to prove they are worthy of love.

The second temptation or common wound among EAS casualties is trying to compensate for lack of inner worth by collecting degrees, certificates and qualifications. These external validations are intended to compensate for internal insecurity; i.e., you may not love me but you will respect me for my achievements. It's true. People will respect you. But it's the wrong reason to achieve. Think the Devil didn't try this one on Jesus for size? He did.

With the second temptation Satan strikes at the heart of a hoped-for weakness. In Luke 4:6 he offers authority and glory (really terrific external validations, to be sure) if Jesus will worship him. Power and glory in the world's eyes carries popularity and influence, but having his Father's blessing means Jesus can live without the world's power and glory. The same is true of us. What freedom it is to live at peace, not needing others to validate you! Someone who can live without needing "approval" (because they already have it) is truly free to lead others. Paul echoes this truth in Galatians 1:10: "Am I trying to please man? If I were still trying to please man, I would not be a servant of Christ."

Like Jesus, Paul knew he was pleasing God, so he could act in ways not conditioned by man's approval or disapproval.

In Luke 6:26 (the Beatitudes) Jesus calls out the risk of being addicted to approval. "Woe to you, when all people speak well of you!" It is important to note that Jesus is not saying "Woe if people speak well of you." He is talking about your needing *everyone* to speak well of you. Affirmation is generally a positive grace in one's life, except when you have to have it from everyone.

The woe happens when you are meeting everyone's expectations, for then you have surrendered leadership to become a follower. You are at everyone's beck and call. You've become a people-pleaser. This is a place of deep inner disquiet. Needing something at any cost is a primary symptom of addiction.

You will never have done enough because you can never really know how much is enough or who will suddenly have a new expectation of you. Exhaustion laps around the edges of your life waiting to eventually drown you in fatigue.

Conversely, the power packed into having your father's blessing settles the issue of your worth. Some people may not like what you do, or decisions you make, but the impact of that on your personhood cannot pierce you to the core and injure you.

Satan's final temptation again questions Jesus' identity as the Son of God, and again calls for him to prove to others that he is powerful and invulnerable. (Loose translation: "Go ahead and jump from the pinnacle of the Temple right down into that canyon below. If you're the Son of God you won't get hurt!" (Matthew 4:5 Luke 4:9). Once again we see Jesus demonstrating freedom in his ministry as the result of having had his affirmation cup filled to the brim before starting out to do his work. He was free to resist the temptation to prove his personal worth to others. He didn't react *inwardly* (cringing inside or getting defensive) when he was challenged; he acted *outwardly*, directly confronting the conflict. Jesus refused to link his identity with powerful action because he had nothing to prove. His father had settled the issue of Jesus' identity as a loved and affirmed Son at his Baptism in the River Jordan.

4

Contrasting Jesus' Behaviors

In his last-ditch try at tempting Jesus, the Devil was attempting to fuse Jesus' performance together with his worth as a person, so that Jesus' performance would define him. It failed with Jesus of course. Sadly, however, many of us have had performance and worth fused together in our family of origin, and that has robbed us of the ability to confront conflict like Jesus did.

The symptoms of EAS are listed below. We shall be dealing with each in the course of this book:

- Conflict avoidance

- Feelings of unworthiness

- Feeling of inferiority

- Feelings of not belonging in groups

- Undue subjectivity [4]

---

[4] This is a term you may not have encountered, so it's worth a footnote. *Subjectivity* refers to how someone's judgment has been shaped by personal *feelings* instead of outside influences. It is a form of bias and is the opposite of objectivity, which is based purely on the facts and isn't personal. We expect law judges to put aside their subjectivity and make decisions based on objectivity.

- Obsessive need for approval
- Confusion when affirmation is given
- Discounting affirmation when given
- Approval evaporating quickly
- People-pleasing
- Not having a regular day off
- Perfectionism and overworking
- Being critical of others' work habits
- Resentment at not being appreciated
- Exhaustion / Flirting with burnout
- Anxiety
- Insecurity

A Psychiatrist's Take

This list of symptoms does not fit clearly into any of the standard psychiatric diagnoses described in the American Psychiatric Association's Diagnostic and Statistical Manual-V. The closest diagnosis this list of symptoms comes to in the DSM-V would be that of either Personality Traits or a Personality Disorder. A Personality Disorder is defined as "an enduring pattern of inner experience and behavior that deviates markedly from the expectations of the individual's culture, is pervasive and inflexible, has an onset in adolescence or early adulthood, is stable over time, and leads to distress or impairment." (p.645)

DSM-V distinguishes between Personality Disorders and Personality Traits, which are less severe in nature.

"Personality traits are enduring patterns of perceiving, relating to, and thinking about the environment and oneself that are exhibited in a wide range of social and personal contexts. Only when personality traits are inflexible and maladaptive and cause significant functional impairment or subjective distress do they constitute personality disorders." (p. 647)

External Affirmation Syndrome (EAS) could be described in some people as dealing with Personality Traits and in some others as closer to what DSM-V describes as a Personality Disorder. There is often much room for opinion and subjectivity in deciding whether an individual has Personality Traits or a Personality Disorder. For practical purposes then the most important issue related to whether one fits the definition of EAS (and therefore should get help) is whether he or she feels there is any significant functional impairment or subjective distress from the described symptoms.

Jim Stanley, M.D.

We will find stark differences when we compare and contrast the record of Jesus' performance in his earthly life with that of an EAS sufferer:

Conflict Avoidance

When someone wants affirmation from another they will avoid irritating or annoying that person. Conflict avoidance is at the far end of a spectrum, the other end of which is tolerating conflict, as Jesus demonstrated so well in his earthly ministry. An EAS sufferer lives life at or near one end of this spectrum – the wrong end. Typically they will admit they do not like conflict. "Yes, it really distresses me when someone crosses me even just a little." You can imagine how distressed they can be when someone is actually angry with them.

Jesus' behaviors exemplified the opposite of conflict avoidance. About one-third of the Gospel narratives deal with various disputes between Jesus and the reigning religious authorities, the Sadducees and the Pharisees. Jesus, confident in his worth in the Father's eyes, was able to stand his ground and push back against both evil forces and corrupt human institutions. He infuriated religious leaders. He broke through their boundaries; for example creating a furor by healing on the Sabbath. He stepped squarely into a conflict with scribes and Pharisees intent on stoning a woman caught in adultery, confronting them with a direct challenge: "Let him who is without sin among you be the first to throw a stone at her" (John 8:7).

Feelings of unworthiness or not belonging never characterized Jesus. He is recorded in John's Gospel as defining himself with various "I AMs" – I am the Bread of Life, I am the Good Shepherd, I am the Living Water, I am the Resurrection, etc. Having been affirmed by his Father he clearly knew his worth and was confident to name it publicly.

As for group participation, Jesus assembled a group that would stay together for the rest of their lives and change the world. He spoke emphatically about this group: "You are my disciples." (Affirmation, right?) He was at the center of the team and he belonged to it. His group would define themselves by his name.

Jesus was not prone to subjectivity. He did not take things personally. He was objective, as in his discerning of the motives of people's hearts. His one moment of taking things personally was in Gethsemane. The man Jesus felt the pain of abandonment by his team, and in anguish cried out: "So, could you not watch with me one hour?" (Matthew 26:40).

Despite horrendous abuse, Jesus didn't take things personally because he wasn't in need of affirmation. He deflected accusations. They bounced off him. Unlike Jesus an EAS sufferer cannot deflect personal attacks, so the toxin-tipped arrows of accusation can pierce deeply to administer their poison.

Jesus' power to deflect is evident even at the time of his greatest stress (John 18:33-37). On trial before Pilate, who hurls a questioning accusation: "Are you the King of the Jews?" Jesus responds objectively, not subjectively:

29

"Do you say this of your own accord, or did others say it to you about me?" Exasperated, Pilate fires back, "So you are a King?" Jesus remains objective, keeps his feelings in check, and deflects: "You say that I am a king. For this purpose I was born and for this purpose I have come into the world – to bear witness to the truth. Everyone who is of the truth listens to my voice."

People-pleasing

People-pleasers are destined to find that their activity is exhausting and burnout inevitable.

Jesus wasn't a people-pleaser. He didn't let himself be pulled off course by other's felt needs, despite his ability to meet them. He was more strategic than that. He would not soft-pedal the Kingdom to accommodate a potential newcomer and was even willing to send someone away disappointed, as with the Rich Young Man of Matthew 19. There are other examples, as in Luke 22 where Jesus is confronted with harsh words when brought before the Chief Priests and Scribes: "If you are the Christ, tell us." But Jesus said, "If I tell you, you will not believe . . ."

His answers were far from pleasing to the ear and sealed his earthly fate. Being true to himself was his guiding principle, not being a people-pleaser. In Luke 4 he tells people with huge expectations that he will not be staying in town to heal their sick, that he must go elsewhere, disappointing those pressing him to stay. An EAS sufferer would have squeezed in another half-dozen healing appointments in order not to disappoint people who were depending on him. Jesus even resisted the demands of hurting masses. In one example he devises an exit strategy to escape the pressure and demands of a crowd. He has the disciples find a boat and takes off in it across the sea, leaving behind the unmet needs of sick and hurting people. It is true that he had worked hard all day healing and teaching all who sought him, but the next day he takes the whole day off to go on a mountain retreat (Luke 5:16; Matthew 14:23).

At this point you might be thinking, "Hey wait a minute, I thought Jesus had compassion for people. Why would he turn them away again and again like that?"

True to himself Jesus put his mission first place in his life, and that mission was to do the work the father sent him to accomplish (John 5:36). He explained it this way: "We must work the works of him who sent me while it is day; night is coming, when no one can work. As long as I am in the world, I am the light of the world." (John 9:4,5)

No Sabbath Days Off

There's a reason for the signs posted in passenger aircraft advising you to secure your own oxygen mask before attending to your child's mask. Your greater obligation is to ensure that you will be able to discharge that responsibility. We just saw the principle at work in Jesus taking care that he would be able to do the work the Father assigned him.

So it was with Jesus, and so it is with us. He kept a weekly Sabbath. EAS folk generally do not, which is plain foolishness. They remind you of the proverbial cobbler whose children go barefoot because of his obsession with making more shoes.

For nearly twenty years now, seven times each year, I have led a team hosting *Oasis Retreats* for clergy who have burned out. A common denominator of the participants over all these years is their failure to take any regular "Sabbath" day off to rest. The need of a regular, uninterrupted full day off is lost on an EAS person. In the case of clergy the reason is clear enough. Rest-days taken off earn little or no affirmation from most parishioners. Instead, clergy sense they are rewarded for the extra hospital visit made or the additional meeting attended. Unfortunately, their Pastor being unavailable for a full day every single week isn't widely approved by congregants. They may give intellectual assent to the idea as being Biblical. But if Pastor doesn't visit them in the hospital, see them in his office, or attend their Bible Study, watch out. Sabbath rest is no defense to such criticism, or at least so runs the clergy mind. I cite the clergy only as an example. An EAS person in any line of professional work is very vulnerable to, if not actually defenseless against, similar kinds of real or imagined pressures.

Perfectionism and Overwork

Working long and hard hours does not in and of itself earn affirmation, or so the EAS person thinks. No, all the work has to be perfect. The more perfect the work the greater affirmation one should get from it and, one could assume, without criticism.

Wrong! Even if you do everything perfectly in your own eyes there will always be that someone who sees what they regard as a mistake, or a necessary improvement, or risks and downsides associated with your plans.

Perfectionism and excessive work carry definite consequences: anxiety, insecurity, resentment for not being appreciated, and even your own criticism toward others who don't want to work as hard as you do. Anxiety creeps in about whether the work is good enough or whether you have done enough. There is always more work than you have time for, and of course the more skilled you are the more in demand you become. There is anxiety that comes to you as you lie awake at night reviewing what was accomplished that day, what needs to be done tomorrow, and how it will be received. "Received" is code for affirmed. Will I be told I am okay? Will my stock rise higher after this project is completed? Oh, and I set the bar so high in my previous projects that it keeps on getting harder for me to perform.

Resentment

Here and there, maybe in the wee hours of the night, resentment creeps in . . . Why do they expect so much of me? Why don't they have the same high expectations of others? They just don't realize the hours I'm putting in! No, I'm not rewarded for all I do! And once more they've gone and messed up my painstaking planning!

33

Now watch out, Dear Reader, here comes something *insidious*[5] – An EAS sufferer readily sees the splinter in another's eye but doesn't even suspect the existence of the mote in his own eye! Why? Because "they" are useful to him; they let him hide from his condition while blaming others for the hurt in his life. Here is a downward spiral that will not end well. Mercifully, the EAS sufferer can be helped out of this condition, aas we shall see.

---

[5] *Insidious* means developing so gradually as to be well established before becoming apparent.

5

Subjectivity

Subjectivity is most readily comprehended when it is compared to its opposite: objectivity. When a person is objective they are unbiased, their reactions are not much colored by feelings or previous experiences, so they are able to be pretty clear-headed. On the other hand, life in the subjectivity lane is a hellish one because that person isn't free to be emotionally clear headed. Their perceptions are torqued (twisted out of shape) by feelings and their previous experiences. EAS sufferers are stuck here trying to live out their relationships with the other people in their lives.

On a scale of one to ten (one being very *subjective* and ten being *objective*) healthy people live pretty close to objectivity. I think most clinicians would agree it's best to be in the eight-to-nine range on the scale, responding to happenings objectively so far as possible. For example, if someone you know passes right by you without looking at you or stopping to chat, the objective person would, eight or nine times out of ten, say to themselves something like: "Wonder what's wrong with her today. She's sure preoccupied or maybe having a bad time right now!" Not so EAS folk. They live in the one-to-four range on our scale. They'll pretty invariably take personally a situation like this and internalize it. "Did I say something inappropriate? What have I gone and done now?"

Subjectivity is indicative of an unhealthy enmeshment in one's relationships, a caring too much about what others may think, or being preoccupied with how others view you.

The EAS person hasn't fully *individuated*. This means they have not completed the process of growing up to become their own person – so as to be able to stand alone on their own two feet and defend their beliefs and ideas, or even defend themselves. One who hasn't individuated seeks others to validate their personhood. Compare Jesus, who stood alone before Pilate, strong and complete, whether or not Pilate affirmed him.

Addicted To Affirmation

The professional literature has had little to say about External Affirmation Syndrome. I noticed this when it first surfaced about twenty years ago. Although I cannot claim credit for naming EAS I have devoted many years to its study, leading to the conclusions stated in this book.

It is worth repeating that at the center of this therapy is an important metaphor – the *Cup*. We all have such a cup and it needs to be kept pretty much filled up with affirmation in order for us to be healthy and to able to be of any godly service to others. Parents are called by God to fill up a child's cup with words and acts that affirm. But just as starving children will go into the streets to beg, when a person doesn't receive enough affirmation they too may go begging for it. Panhandling with one's cup (offering it *habitually*, even promiscuously) is called External Affirmation Syndrome or EAS. The EAS sufferer, being addicted to affirmation, carries their cup quite openly ("wears it on their sleeve," you could say).

The non-addictive person keeps their cup from view, displaying it cautiously – and only when three (3) factors are well aligned:

- When they themselves have discerned that another has good discernment;[6]
- When the other person knows them well enough to be able to make a constructive judgment;
- When the trusted person speaks with *grace* as well as truth.

Two out of the three above doesn't cut it.

For example, the other person may be your spouse with very good discernment, and their opinion is valued; but today they're in a mood with an edge to it. So this particular day it's only two out of three, and you should keep your cup out of reach because the truth about you is not likely to be seasoned with very much, if any, grace. (Truth not seasoned with grace will hurt you.)

But an unhealthy EAS person, well knowing their spouse is on edge, will go right ahead anyway to seek affirmation for something or other they've accomplished, perhaps even a very small thing, ignoring the risk of a poor result because *neediness* is controlling them.

---

[6] A person has discernment if they have insight into things and good judgment; in other words objectivity and common sense.

Evident Neediness

The evident neediness of EAS folk isn't lost on others, though of course a beggar likely doesn't see himself as a pathetic figure. So EAS sufferers go about seeking affirmation at the risk of losing the respect of others. They may get an offering in their cup but they'll go down in the esteem of the one giving it. What a beggar may take to be affirmation the other person may have given more as a simple pat on the head. This is a very poor balance of trade any way you look at it. Even worse, a beggar will ignore basics like the fact that the one to whom they are offering their cup is not by any stretch a discerning person. A beggar may even place the question of their personal worth in the hands of a relative stranger.

Putting a Hole in the Cup

Consciously or maybe unconsciously an EAS sufferer assumes that their father knew them better than anyone, so his failure to affirm them has left a festering wound. Now, while they're operating on this assumption about their father, along comes someone else (who by this definition can't know them as well) and this person very kindly, and in truth, deposits some affirmation in the cup. How will it be received?

You might surmise with a big thank you, but more usually it will be sloughed-off.

But then in a few minutes there may well be an equal and opposite reaction, though not a public one. The deposit is taken out of the cup to be evaluated. "She just doesn't know me well enough. If she *really* knew me she wouldn't be able to affirm me in the same way." A little hole gets made in the bottom of the cup causing a hemorrhage that worsens the deficit the EAS sufferer is trying to correct. Affirmation evaporates when evaluated in this way. One never gets to savor even a little affirmation when it is taken out of the cup and questioned. Here is *subjectivity* at perhaps its worst – perhaps the most pitiful of all traps the EAS sufferer falls into – because it cancels hope, at least for the time being. There are other ways a hole appears in the cup, as we shall see.

Trevor Walters

6

Affirmation in the Early Years

How does a hole in the cup happen? How did your father or another person puncture yours? I know very well how it happened for me. My father took away the joy in achieving anything, and he replaced it with a ratchet that worked in only one direction, ever upward. When I was about to be able to celebrate an achievement he would raise the carrot or reward beyond reach.

"Well son, that B-plus on your report for Math was okay but perhaps next semester you could work harder and get an A-minus."

Next semester would come with the A- minus in place, but another topic would get the attention. The B-plus in Art really should be an A-minus. Sure, the A-minus in Math was begrudgingly acknowledged, but that left me confused and even feeling shamed.

Over the years I learned that nothing would be good enough to be worthy of my father's affirmation. It took me until I was forty years old to be satisfied with my own accomplishments, to be properly proud of them, and to give myself permission to celebrate success.

Resentment Begins at Home

Resentment begins at home . . . and then it generalizes outward. This is a hard saying, so let's carefully pick it apart.

From a fairly early age if asked whether I was angry with my father I would have denied it, though if pressed I might have owned up to the fact I had a resentment or slow burn towards him, but it was masked by my increasingly greater need of affirmation from him.

Did you, do you, secretly long for your father to wake up and recognize that you, his son or daughter, are a person of worth and that your choices of late have been good choices? I said *of late* because when you were growing up and unable able to please him there came a time in all likelihood when you rebelled or you jolly well wanted to rebel. Maybe you told your father, at least under your breath, "Ha, if you think this is bad, let me show you bad." However, more likely, you simply hung on tight and toughed it out. You couldn't afford to cause him to pull away from you! Indeed, the greater your addiction to affirmation the less likely it is that you would have rebelled then and there.

As put-downs, criticisms, lack of praise, or praise given without enthusiasm, accumulates through the years many adults despair of ever being able to do anything right in their father's eyes. For some it is not that you were actually criticized; you were ignored. So you craved attention and sought it the only way left to you: acting-out negatively. For others your "goodness" was exemplary but you were suspicious of father's affection so you always tried to stay on his good side. Alas, in either case, inner feelings of rejection were the bitter fruit budding and growing on the tree of your childhood.

Bitter Fruit from the Tree of Childhood

As an adult you have feelings (you may not be conscious of them) that there is something unlovable lying deeply hidden within you, a dark secret that must never be probed or uncovered.

Others of you were aware of your siblings playing it rather fast and loose while you, the "good one," never got the attention and affirmation you were looking for. Some of you suffered the indignity of pretty roguish siblings getting more in their cups than you did. You probably pondered over what you were doing wrong for this to be happing to you, but with no obvious conclusion to be drawn other than there must have been something profoundly wrong with you that caused it.

Most of you in the middle of the birth order pretty much kept your heads down in order to remain more or less inconspicuous. Your natural spontaneity (the side of you that would have had you bounding up to a parent to earn their delight, enthusiasm and praise) was quenched. So you learned to avoid conflict by avoiding the limelight and being careful not to speak up. Your proclivities now, as then, are to avoid possible criticism by avoiding being noticed and not seeking after affirmation. You don't see the big deal about recognition, or so you tell yourself, until recognition doesn't come over time and you begin to feel some faint twinges of shame. You are aware you have a rather empty cup and that fact draws you into what amounts to self-condemnation more often than you'll recognize or admit. In truth, getting approval from others is of paramount importance to you, even to the point of crippling you when you do not get it. Yes, you too have a big hole in your cup. Most likely what pierced your cup most was a parent's sharp tongue and/or his or her failure to balance correction with affirmation.

How Childhood Affects Us

So where does the bitter fruit from the tree of your childhood leave you in your personal relationships?

First of all, where does it leave you in intimate friendships? Could it be you've come through the carnage of some, maybe even serial, broken relationships? People may have pushed you away and you've concluded that intimacy can hurt you, though you still long for it. Your experience of rejection tells you your parent must have been right; you are not very loveable, and other people have glimpsed this awful truth too. (It wasn't always your parent using cutting words; they didn't need words with their actions speaking so loudly.)

And where does it leave you with authority figures, a boss or a mentor for example? Somehow they slipped silently and seamlessly into the same dominant role as the father who held such sway over you. Do they now fall short of fulfilling "rightful" expectations? Do they disappoint by not appearing to value you enough? You do your level best to get them to see how much you're accomplishing but they don't reward you according to what you feel you deserve. Ah, but there is good news for you despite all that because there really is a way out of this unbroken circle, as we'll see.

Most important of all, where does that bitter childhood fruit leave you with God? Since you did not get the affirmation you needed from your earthly father, I suspect you are experiencing a distance in your relationship with God. More exactly, you are insecure about where you stand with God. Now this is a vital topic, though it is beyond the scope of this book. You may get some important clues to your relationship with God as you take back control of who you allow to deposit affirmation in your cup.

People's problems about God have various causes, but for purposes of our focus here it may come down to feelings of betrayal. With God being presented as a father figure, "Once bitten, twice shy" may apply in your case. A difficult or missing earthly father can make a person distrustful of father figures, while in another person it may cause cravings for a close relationship with God. People do have choices. My best advice: "Draw near to God, and he will draw near to you" (James 4:8). If that doesn't register sufficiently with you, get a Spiritual Director to help you.

Trevor Walters

7

Who Controls Your Cup?

The previous chapter's three questions about your relationship with intimate friendships, with authority figures, and God may have left you feeling that you yourself are the common denominator. Such being the case why would you ever dig-around in your childhood just to revisit the site of bad happenings? Surely excavating that pit would only bring face-to-face encounters with your feelings of hurt or worthlessness. Why would anyone want to go back to a damaged childhood to exhume the little body they buried there . . . or thought they buried?

C.S. Lewis told the story of a childhood toothache in the context of his fear of the dentist: should he tell his parents who would take him there . . . or not? Finally pain drove him to tell them, the tooth was fixed, and life resumed anew. It's rather like that with you except you've buried your pain and seldom feel its motivation. But it doesn't change the fact that your "tooth" is *festering* (In medicine: becoming an increasing source of irritation or poisoning) whether you realize it or not. To use another medical term you have an *occult condition*, meaning hidden and unseen but very real.

You know rationally that any child is like a sponge that

absorbs the environment they are placed into. Love the child and they cannot help believing they are loveable. Withhold love and the child will come to believe they are unlovable.

I think you should be getting my second opinion on your childhood precisely for the reason that your anger (or your aversion to anger) protests too much. Your anger shouts out that your father acted unfairly. Your heart cries out "this child deserved to be *loved*!"

In this chapter we'll be exploring together your growing-up years. But first, for those of you with *reverse order syndrome* (people who compulsively go to the back of a book to read it first), let me make things a little easier for you. You felt a mixture of emotions when leaving home, your own family of origin home, shedding the sins of your parents like old clothes (or so you thought). There was a note of grief, realizing you never heard the healing words you longed for: "This is my dearly beloved son (daughter) in whom I am well pleased." However, there was a little tingle of excitement too, "Hey, I'm starting off with a clean slate. For the first time the jury is out on my value as a person." What seemed like an open and shut case against you suddenly looks like it could go either way, if others perceive actual worth in you.

Okay, that's a pretty normal reaction but here comes the difference maker: where are you going to keep the cup that was so empty when you started your new life outside the home of origin? More exactly, are you going to guard it very carefully? Are you or are you not actually in control of your cup?

Now that it looks like a real possibility that some people in your life could begin putting affirmation into your cup (with you believing they really mean it, too) it is your responsibility to associate with people whose discernment you have good reason to believe is trustworthy. The corollary is true too. Insofar as it is up to you to do so, you should keep away from critical folks with poor discernment. There are always times when being around people like that is unavoidable, in which case you must be careful to keep your cup to yourself and not give them a chance to have a go at it.

Protecting Your Cup

Many cases of clergy burnout result from their wearing the affirmation cup on their sleeves. Unlike those in other walks of life clergy cannot so easily get away from critical people. Clergy are called, ordained, and expected to care for all who are in their charge, no matter people's foibles. St. Paul cautioned clergy to guard their cup in ministry. He knew that no one is able to lead successfully if they need to keep everyone happy.

> "Am I now seeking the approval of man, or of God? Or am I trying to please man? If I were still trying to please man, I would not be a servant of Christ." (Galatians 1:10)

When your cup is "out there" on your sleeve you are totally vulnerable to critical people whose pseudo-vocation seems to be pouring toxic waste into other people's cups. What you desperately need is a new kind of freedom when in the company of others – freedom from reacting with your same-old-same-old subjective ways of internalizing – becoming hurt, defensive, and resentful.

Now some will say of it, "Isn't this all just self-centered naval gazing? For crying out loud just get over it and move on." Not so fast, I say. In fact I would say begging for affirmation like you did in your home of origin was intensely self-centered behavior.

Your fixation was trying to be liked, stroked, and praised. That made you touchy, prickly, and sensitive.

The vision of healthy new behaviors is one where the old-self, with its resentment and pre-occupations, is in the process of being crucified with Christ. It was and remains open to you to accept as your new behavior pattern:

> "I have been crucified with Christ. It is no longer I who live, but Christ who lives in me. And the life I now live in the flesh I live by faith in the Son of God, who loved me and gave himself for me." (Galatians 2:20)

With the old co-dependences broken you can move on from being stuck in a bad place. You are set free as a butterfly. Now and forever Jesus has the preeminence when it comes to filling your cup.

8

Spring Training

Major League baseball teams conduct a series of practices and exhibition games to get ready for the next baseball season. They call it spring training. College football teams hold spring practice in the offseason too. In either sport the players get themselves into shape, shake-off shortcomings of previous seasons, sharpen skills, maybe put some new wrinkles into their game, and get ready to start afresh in a brand-new unblemished season. All this is done under careful tutelage of coaches who know the sport from the inside out, who also know a player's upside potential and their besetting bad habits. So let's take a page from the world of sports training for a brief timeout to catch our breath, reinforce some learning, and get ready with a good roadmap in our lap before setting off on the next legs of our journey to healing and deliverance.

To recap an overview:

- The usual cause of EAS among men and women in the professions and other high-functioning occupations is the failure of their fathers to bestow his unconditional blessing and affirmation.

- One's *cup* represents their repository for approval and affirmation. One's parents are called by God to fill a child's cup with words and acts that affirm them. A hole is made in the cup when a parent withholds affirmation. Not feeling good about one's successes, and therefore about oneself, widens the hole and stains the cup.

- Children whose parents (most especially their fathers) failed this responsibility will develop a chronic need of affirmation so great they will go about begging affirmation from almost anyone.

- Sadly, a father's failure to affirm poisons the well; affirmation given by others won't be accepted at face value. "If my father who really knew me could not affirm me, then this person's affirmation cannot be valid. They really don't know me."

The main behaviors of EAS sufferers:

- They are unaware that habitually seeking after affirmation is pulling them along the path toward a midlife burnout (emotional and mental exhaustion).

- They are prone to *subjectivity* in that their reactions to daily happenings, perceptions, beliefs and emotions are focused inwardly, inside their own minds. They have become preoccupied with how others may view them, and they can take trivial happenings personally.

- They are conflict-averse, so that they will habitually avoid conflict in order to preserve the opportunity to obtain some affirmation. They tend to become chronic people-pleasers.

- People who do not have their father's blessing settle for their own worth as measured by *performance*.

- Thinking that more and better work will bring affirmation the EAS sufferer becomes a workaholic perfectionist who doesn't practice regular "Sabbath" days off from work.

- Failing to garner the affirmation they feel is due them, EAS sufferers will experience insecurity and anxiety and manifest anger and resentment.

The roadmap for our journey to healing and deliverance has its stopping-off places. Places that like C.S. Lewis' trip to the dentist are not without discomforts. To this I say *no-pain-no-gain*. I'll merely list some here. Then we'll take it all up in the chapters that follow.

- Assessment of what your parents did about their responsibility to fill your cup

- Compiling a list of offences against you

- Forgiving versus excusing your parents

- Assigning offences to the rightful person

- Taking charge of your cup

- Leaving the home of origin with your cup

- Letting Jesus fill your cup

- Letting others fill your cup

- Drinking from the cup

- Sharing the contents of your cup with others

- Parenting yourself

The next stage in this therapy will be to inquire into how it was that your parents went about their parental obligation to affirm you. We will be looking to see whether affirmation was conditioned on your behavior or whether it was based upon your individual worth as a person. Was it earned or freely given? Were there differences in affirmation as apportioned to your siblings?

With a listing of your parents' shortcomings in hand the next level in therapy will be about bringing to consciousness the impact of these parental failings on your own sense of worth. The reason for this inquiry is that no one can truly forgive an injury unless they know the fullness of it. Only with adequate knowledge in hand is anyone prepared to make a godly decision to forgive. Here comes something that may be new to you: making a decision to forgive and actually forgiving are two different things, just as preparing to undertake a journey and completing the trip are two different things. And the longer and more arduous the journey the more one has to prepare for it – if there is to be a good outcome.

This is the pivotal place where we discern whether parental offences have been forgiven (which is health-giving for you) or merely excused (buried and festering). To clarify the essential distinction between forgiving and excusing, we will be defining forgiveness and resentment and looking into the domino effect of merely excusing.

At our next stopping-off place in the healing journey we'll rehearse what you are going to be hauling back to your parents' house. Oh-oh, alarm bells just sounded inside you, didn't they?

Do I have to get my parents involved in this therapy?

No, your parents are no longer the problem.

What is tripping you up are the gut twinges when you think of your home of origin or the parental images that keep playing like videos in your head. At issue for you now are memories of not being affirmed and being made to feel unworthy as a consequence. The task at hand is convincing yourself that you can live a healthy life without your parents' affirmation. To best accomplish this we are simply going to *imagine* going back home again toting some reeking garbage bags . . . and leaving without them.

Mourning a lost childhood is the next step in your healing process. This means mourning your losses from not being affirmed; also mourning for your parents, who tragically missed out on celebrating the uniqueness of how God made you and gave you into their care. Rehearsing how you would see your parents reacting to the charges against them follows.

Managing the various permutations that an encounter with your parents could bring is the next challenge. And when there is no more to be said or done, it is time to leave your parents house and let go.

Before leaving it can prove most fruitful to ask your parents if they know where your cup is. No, not the utilitarian cup you've had all these years but a unique, beautiful cup that God made especially for you and has always wanted you to have and treasure. Often parents do know and will offer directions to find it. It may be gathering dust in a china closet (especially if they're

British). Or it may be buried in the garden. In one of my recent counseling sessions a fellow saw it hanging on his father's belt.

With your God-given cup in hand you will be coached to leave that house – to close its door as a deliberate action to confirm the closing of a chapter in your life. Now it's time to begin a new life, with a pristine cup. At this point in the journey the first person to whom I ask people to offer their cup is Jesus. When I ask them (dozens of them over the years), "What do you think Jesus would like to pour into your cup?" they always know the answer. It will be something deeply affirming, something that seals the reality of Jesus' blessing resting on them.

This is the seminal moment of the painful journey, a powerful moment because we're at home now with our Father:

> "The sure provisions of my God attend me all
> my days; O may Thy house be my abode, and
> all my work be praise. There would I find a
> settled rest, while others go and come; No
> more a stranger, nor a guest, but like a child at
> home."[7]

The new cup is too precious to wear on the sleeve. It is time to manage it carefully. It's time to guard it, and time to risk it with others. It is time to allow yourself, as a ritual every evening, to savor what was put into your cup that day. Remember, one is blessed in order to be a blessing

---

[7] Isaac Watts (1674-1748) based on the 23rd Psalm.

to others. Blessing others is the mandate of the person affirmed by God.

You are now on track to become the *wounded healer,* anointed by God to be a blessing to others.[8]

A Psychiatrist's Take

The author uses two main therapeutic techniques in treating External Affirmation Syndrome symptoms: They are called *psychodynamic psychotherapy* and *cognitive-behavioral* therapy. Both of these are widely accepted in the broad psychological and psychiatric communities.

Psychodynamic psychotherapy us used to help the patient understand the connection between parent-child relationships and their current feelings and beliefs. Understanding how repetitive childhood experiences can shape adult attitudes is often helpful as a first step in modifying maladaptive attitudes and behavior.

Using cognitive-behavioral therapy the patient is directed to focus on certain beliefs and behaviors and to consider whether these beliefs and behaviors are rational. Visualization of past experiences can help the patient

---

[8] A term originated by Carl Jung and taken up by others, including Henri Nouwen. The idea is that one's own woundedness can be a source of strength and healing in counseling others.

understand where inappropriate attitudes, behavioral patterns, and negative feelings may have originated. The understanding gained in this way can serve to help the patient modify irrational beliefs and behaviors.

Jim Stanley, M.D.

9

Don't Take the Fifth

The fifth amendment to the United States Constitution is a part of the Bill of Rights and protects people from being forced to testify against themselves in a criminal case. In popular American culture "taking the Fifth" is a lighthearted way of saying you're not going to answer a question. When you say "I'm taking the fifth on that," it means "Hey, don't ask me about that stuff." It's a parody of the Bill of Rights of course, as perhaps most people in the United States know.

Okay, you're asking what this has to do with EAS. Well, there's another Fifth that gets parody treatment too, only the result here is unintended and the consequences damaging. This one springs from misunderstanding the genuine article – in this case, the Fifth of the Ten Commandments:

> "Honor your father and your mother, that your
> days may be long in the land that the Lord your
> God is giving you." (Exodus 20:12)

Our context is forgiveness of one's parents; however, forgiveness must be grounded in truth, i.e., based on a truthful understanding of the extent of the trespass and damage that needs to be forgiven. Before they have had sound teaching in this area people often interpret the Fifth Commandment to mean they can't say anything derogatory about their parents to anyone else, including their priest, pastor, psychologist or psychiatrist. To do so in this view would be to dishonor their parents in violation of the Commandment. People feel guilty about sharing parental failures despite their confidence that their memory is accurate as to the facts of their parents' failing to affirm them. And when people do allow themselves to speak freely to me about the sins of their parents, they have an immediate need to tell me their parents' good points too.

Here are the kinds of responses I get when probing people who are sensitive to the Fifth Commandment's directive to "Honor your father and your mother" . . . but who misapprehend it to their own harm:

- They will react to my questions very defensively. Sometimes there is even a hostile reaction in order to protect a parent they feel may be falling victim to my persecution.

- They will focus mainly on the good aspects of the parenting, with a small detour to the subject of their parents' shortcomings – then and there followed up by making excuses for them.

- Some will speak at length about their parents' poor parenting, followed by a non-sequitur declaration that they were quite good parents.

- Those more aware of the underlying need to honor their parents will often say (after listing negative experiences in childhood) that they feel very bad about sharing these things. They may conclude with something like "Please don't hate my parents or think badly of them."

- Fewer will say, "I feel as though I am dishonoring my parents," but then proceed to speak openly and honestly about their parents' shortcomings.

Clarifying The Fifth Commandment

By now you realize our chapter heading means don't take the Fifth Commandment *in vain*. Pretending that people's sins don't exist doesn't honor them and is not honoring of God. So, in ministering to hurting EAS people, how can we help them to get through their Fifth Commandment roadblock?

- **Often a question or two works to loosen the grip of muddled thinking.**

    Ask "Does it honor someone to tell lies about them?" "Does your preserving in a distorted or redacted history honor your father or mother?" "Shouldn't we go about honoring what is honorable and just call a spade a spade as to the rest of it?"

- **Invite consideration of the *Covenant Expectations* of parents and children found in the Bible.**

    "Children, obey your parents in everything, for this pleases the Lord. Fathers, do not provoke your children, lest they become discouraged." (Colossians 3:20, 21)

At this stage in the life of EAS sufferers they are no longer children, nor are you asking them to disobey their parents. A Biblical covenant has two parties, each with their reciprocal obligations. For example:

> "If my people who are called by my name humble themselves, and pray and seek my face and turn from their wicked ways, then I will hear from heaven and will forgive their sin and heal their land." (2 Chronicles 7:14)

Given that your parents did not fulfill their side of the Biblical parental covenant, you are quite free to have a confidential conversation about it with a spiritual director or psychological counselor. You will need to reach an accurate understanding of what happened when you were in your home of origin in order to determine the truth about your relationship with your parents. Only then will you be in any position to forgive them. Or you will muddle along not knowing the difference between the forgiveness that brings freedom and merely excusing your parents' poor behavior, which is a festering wound.

- **Invite examination of how Jesus interacted with children.**

It is enlightening and liberating to see how Jesus honored children. The children in Matthew 19:14 were probably making a fuss or competing for his attention, so the disciples shushed them. But Jesus said,

> "Let the little children come to me and do not hinder them, for to such belongs the kingdom of heaven." (Matthew 19:14)

Here we find Jesus advocating listening to the children as a means of according them equal value to adults. Not hindering them outranks our adult need of peace, quiet and decorum. Jesus took child abuse very seriously:

> "Whoever causes one of these little ones who believe in me to sin, it would be better for him to have a great millstone fastened around his neck and to be drowned in the depth of the sea." (Matthew 18:6)

Other translations read "offend one of these," referring to the damage that can be done to children. Jesus knows their vulnerability and how easily they are wounded. Clearly in his understanding an offended child has rights and needs that are far above an offending adult's rights and needs. In the verses immediately preceding this account Jesus puts a small child into the center of the circle and proceeds to say that in order to enter the Kingdom of God we must humble ourselves like this little child. So, if people in counseling speak humbly of their experiences at the hands of father or mother, God will honor them for honoring their parent. Stated another way, honoring father and mother involves both humility in keeping one's parents in the role of authority conferred by God, while at the same time acknowledging in truth the fact that they failed to live up to the responsibilities of godly parenting.

- **Dispel the notion of carrying a "bad gene."**

  The Book of Ezekiel speaks helpfully to the person who believes that honoring one's parents includes carrying their sins around as some kind of a family curse:

  > "The son shall not suffer for the iniquity of the father, nor the father suffer for the iniquity of the son. The righteousness of the righteous shall be upon himself, and the wickedness of the wicked shall be upon himself." (Ezekiel 18:20)

  The Bible could not be clearer than that, but despite removing the cognitive inhibitions to carrying a parent's sin, the emotional blocks can refuse to dissolve. An approach I employ to address the resistance of an EAS sufferer to speak accurately (and thus truthfully) about their growing up years is to get them to see the shortcomings or sins of a parent as "one step removed."

Maybe Take a Sidestep?

If EAS people can't see a parental failure as being an offense against them selves maybe they can see it through another's eyes, say their mother's eyes. For example, I counseled a man whose parents were both medical doctors. The father spent vast amounts of time away from home saving the world, time that he should have spent to save his son from emotional neglect. How could I get this fellow to see that his own affirmation needs were just as important as any ministry his father was doing out there in the world?

I noticed a small chink in the armor. Whereas the father was absent most of the time healing the world the mother had decided to limit her medical practice to mornings only. The fellow reported that his mother felt neglected if not abandoned by her husband and frustrated at having to function as a single parent. I asked him to journal the ways the father's excessive work had hurt the wife and mother, and to tell me what advice he would have for his father about his neglect of the marriage? This approach gave the son permission to address the same issues that he had with his father. He could see very clearly how his father's poor boundaries had nearly destroyed the marriage. He could accurately name his father's mistakes in balancing marriage with professional life. The son's emotional block of not being able to see that his own needs growing up were a priority suddenly evaporated, along with the all excuses he had been providing for his father. The father's sin of neglect was now a painful reality that could be addressed by an act of forgiveness, and not left festering to define the son's life and curtail his ministry to others.

Trevor Walters

10

Sponge Bob (and Bobette)

Young children define themselves based on their interaction with their parents. Let me say it again, as it is worth repeating: *Kids define themselves* based on interacting with their parents. Young children are very subjective and haven't developed a capacity for objectivity. Keeping an emotional scrapbook of tidbits concerning their personal worth is what they do and what they will take to heart. Emotionally they are sponge-like in absorbing the coloration and tone of their environment. If they are loved they feel worthy of love. If they are ignored they feel unworthy of love. If they are often treated impatiently they will come to believe they are congenitally irritating. If they are afforded great patience they may soon believe they are such valuable people the world will give them deference.

The Principle of Attribution

Parents need to pour what they say carefully and not spill (especially not in anger) because Sponge Boy or Sponge Girl will soak it up in either case. Children do not understand the daily back-and-forth with parents to be a product of situational stress; much less does it give them real insight into their parents' character. They just go along day to day collecting bits and pieces of material for their emotional "scrapbook," pasting together of bits and pieces to make a picture that will tip them one way or another in sensing their emergent worth as a person.

Not everything parents do or say is poured out thoughtfully and carefully, as they would wish. So let's have a look at spillage (parental lapses due to frustration or anger) and what can be done about it. Now here comes the thing about this: Young children can be taught not to internalize a parent's abhorrent behavior. They can learn to re-attribute it to their parents, assuming of course that is where the responsibility rightly rests. Pay attention now because this learning happens only if the parent, after behaving badly, owns the bad moment by telling the child it wasn't the child's fault. "I'm sorry I lost my temper, honey. It wasn't really the spilled juice but Mommy's impatience that caused me to shout like that." "Daddy was thinking about work, I guess, and that's why I didn't pay attention when you were trying to tell me what happened."

Sometimes parenting is about adding a nuance to balance the child's perception: "Mommy was right to tell you to eat with your mouth closed, but she was not right to get irritated!" This form of interaction helps a child to distinguish between what is yours and what is mine.

Meet the Tiger

Lest you think this is too abstract to work in the real world of parenting, let me add a story from when our daughter was six years old. My wife Julie had been quite diligent in her parenting in terms of taking responsibility for her own behavior in order to keep Sarah from internalizing what wasn't hers to own. Nonetheless one day Julie just lost it. She was mad with Sarah! After a little break in the action Sarah stopped what she was doing, looked up at her mother, shook her head and said in an animated voice, "Sometimes I say to myself, is this a Mummy or a T-I-G-E-R!" (We'll be meeting this Tiger again.)

There were two quick reactions to Sarah's pronouncement: Julie collapsed in a heap of laughter, having gotten a huge reality check. Much more importantly six-year old Sarah had sloughed off absorbing any responsibility for her mother's explosion. I feel a little guilty relating the story because I was more often the one to have some anger issues. But the episode speaks very well of a mother's overall body of work in the field of *re-attribution* education.

Not everyone is as proficient as was Sarah's mother when it comes to accepting the responsibility for parenting mistakes. She carefully protected Sarah from gluing any blame that wasn't hers into that little scrapbook of the mind. Some of my own most powerful memories of childhood are of my father trying to apologize for his excesses in reacting to me. It nearly killed him to admit he had made a mistake but somehow he managed to restore relationship or minimize my anger at real or perceived injustices.

If I could give but two gifts to a child the first would be affirmation and the second would be the ability to deflect the bad stuff other people project onto him or her. Or more simply put, the skill to return that garbage from whence it came – to the Tiger.

EAS sufferers have a deep resistance to revisiting their childhood because even at a tender age they were already accepting the responsibility for their parents' shortcomings. (Why would I dig up my dealings with my parents when it was my flawed character that was the problem?)

The Victim as *Perpetrator*

Let me show you an upside down world even worse than "First the sentence, then the trial" in *Alice in Wonderland*. There actually is a mentality where the innocent victim thinks they and not the perpetrator are largely to blame for the crime. Understanding this phenomenon is central to External Affirmation Syndrome therapy.

Shame is the driver of this perversity. The acceptance of shame by the victim is perhaps best seen in the sin of sexual abuse. The victim is abused by the perpetrator's violent lust or desire for power through control. The perpetrator may leave the scene of the crime with little or no remorse. Illogically perhaps, but nonetheless true, the sin attaches to the victim who now owns and carries it in the guise or form of shame. In more than 30 years of counseling I have asked victims of abuse what percentage of responsibility they take for the abuse.[9] To my initial surprise and amazement I discovered that innocent victims take 50% to 100% of the responsibility for being violated. Even in cases where the victim was only about 6 years old at the time of the abuse I have seen them take 90% of the responsibility for the event while assigning their abuser only 10%.

Why this seeming irrationality?

Because victims end up feeling they could have acted differently in the circumstance, or somehow could have stopped the abuse, or that their low worth is a magnet for sin, they'll go through life wearing the shame of it as an invisible tattoo of the soul.

How does this relate to EAS? It is a hard saying but true that shame is the principle fruit of parental failure to bless children with affirmation. You may resist this statement for now but in the end I think you will see it is so.

One of my early homework assignments for EAS people is to ask them to sit in a mall, or park, or at a soccer game to observe children and see that they are indeed sponge-like in any environment. I suggest observing children around six years of age. Why this particular age range? It is because we know intuitively that there is an almost palpable innocence at this age.

---

[9] This is a dangerous question in the hands of the inexperienced, as it has the potential to add to the victim's shame. But when posed by one who intends to battle to remove the shame it becomes a life-giving question.

I ask the client to note the way a child lights up when affirmed and withdraws when criticized or rejected. I ask them to note especially the body language, how a child grows straight when adult praise attends their behavior and how they shrink back when brushed off or put down. I suggest guessing what this or that child may have "clipped" for their mental "scrapbook" to internalize about their value as a person.

The mall, park, or soccer field experience helps to prepare a person for the task of making a written inventory of their own childhood so as to get clarity about "what belongs to me and what belongs to the Tiger." Later on you and I will be returning to your home of origin (an imagined journey, not an actual visit), but not until first you have an understanding of the particulars of your patents' failure to affirm you.

11

Your Affirmation Inventory

When a bad memory from childhood comes to mind, as they will occasionally, people tend to pause for a moment but then move on right away to other things. But such glossing over or minimization as a way of not dealing with emotional wounds doesn't work so well when your hurts are staring right up at you from the written page. In fact gathering hurtful things together in the form of a written inventory makes a case that demands a response. Stated another way, unless you are willing to invest some quality time and energy in making your EAS inventory you will just go about keeping-on-keeping-on, without a change for the better. And how well has that been working for you? So I strongly advise that you pour yourself into this little project.

External Affirmation Inventory

At this point in the book it is a good time to catch up on your EAS paperwork. Make a list of your answers to each of the following categories of questions. This can take some time over at least a couple of days in order to do it well. List all the instances that should be listed in answer to each question. Be as specific as you can because vague doesn't cut it when taking inventory.

About Affirmation

1. In what ways was affirmation withheld?
2. Was affirmation delayed?
3. Was affirmation sometimes given but negated later?
4. Were you affirmed for achievements or for character and attitudes?
5. Were comparisons made between you and your sibling(s)?
6. Did you earn affirmation or was it freely given?
7. How did not getting affirmation wound you?

About Your Parents

1. How were you made to feel special?
2. How were you "celebrated" (e.g., especially on birthdays)?
3. In what ways were you ignored as a child?
4. Did your parents affirm others (children or adults, within or outside the family) more than you?
5. Did your parents usurp your affirmation to their own benefit; e.g., by telling friends or neighbors about your successes but not telling you?
6. What did your parents put in your cup?
7. Did your parents puncture your cup?
8. Were your parents capable of giving affirmation?

About You

1. How did you determine your parents loved you?

2. Do you feel as though you know your parents affirmed you or are you still waiting for it?

3. Do you think that you are ever going to hear that you are beloved by your parents and that they are well pleased with you?

4. Do you wear your cup on your sleeve, looking for affirmation from all and sundry?

5. Are you driven to succeed in order to get people's recognition and respect?

6. In what ways are you carrying too much responsibility on your shoulders?

NOTE: If you don't value yourself highly enough to do this inventory with consummate attention, I'm not very sure you should be reading any further.

Trevor Walters

12

Cheap Forgiveness

The next big leg in our journey is for you to move well beyond excusing your parents and into the freedom that comes from truly forgiving them. Okay, I know you're probably thinking "Oh, for heaven's sake, I have forgiven my father, more than once."

Rest assured that I do believe you have forgiven him, at least for the sins of which you are conscious. But we should define our terms here. To do so we will need to bear in mind a simple but important imperative. Unless you understand the extent of the damage done to you, forgiveness is like a fluttering bird that hasn't found its nest. I call it cheap forgiveness. It may be gracious but what it really amounts to is excusing bad behavior, which is also to say that the person who is the subject of it isn't really forgiven either.

I believe one can forgive only to the degree that one knows the extent of damage inflicted. It is a shocking thing to realize that your whole life until now would have been different if your cup had been filled, in your home of origin.

Ask yourself this: You hear your neighbor drive his car up over your curb and damage your front lawn. You have a good look at it and forgive him, when a little more investigation would reveal that in the course of careening out of control he had run over and killed your family pet.

How much is your forgiveness worth now?

To forgive before fully acknowledging the depths of the damage and pain is entirely inadequate.

To forgive at an emotional level requires feeling the pain of a wound and realizing the consequences of the injury. My definition of forgiveness is this:

> To forgive another is: first, to recognize the extent of the damage they have done; and, second, to hand over to God the "right" to stand in judgment.

If you are a disciple of Jesus Christ –

> "If you forgive the sins of any, they are forgiven them; if you withhold forgiveness from any, it is withheld." (John 20:23)

The effect of forgiving is to offer the trespasser a blessing while simultaneously cleansing your negative emotions that can damage you as much or more as the actual wrong that you suffered.

Resentment is a root of bitterness that leads to a toxic state of your emotional (and I say even physical) health. Therefore, the Bible counsels:

> "Strive for peace with everyone, and for the holiness without which no one will see the Lord. See to it that no one fails to obtain the grace of God; that no "root of bitterness"

springs up and causes trouble, and by it many become defiled." (Hebrews 12:14,15)

The Curse of Excusing

There isn't any debate at this point as to whether yours was a childhood of affirmation, not if you as an EAS sufferer, have carefully done the inventory of your childhood called for in Chapter 11. On the contrary you have decided that your parents sinned in ways that have had a very negative impact on your life to date. So here you are at a fork in the road: What to do about this new or changed view of your parents and their parenting? Do you forgive your parents or do you excuse them?

To excuse is to overlook or make allowances. But it is a very costly option merely to excuse the wrongdoer when what was wrongly done is a sin against you. It amounts to drinking the poison that belongs to the Tiger! This is why the only remedy prescribed in the Bible for sin is forgiveness.

Consider Jesus as he hung on the cross. He said,

"Father, forgive them, for they know not what they do." (Luke 23:43

Here you have it squarely presented. His executioners could have been excused because they knew not they were killing the Christ of God. But even given the availability of this high quality excuse they had to be forgiven.

It is sadly true that we mortals are more prone to excusing sins in place of actually forgiving them – that is, until we have been taught the great difference that forgiveness makes. In my long practice I have heard an absolute multiplicity of excuses offered for parental malpractice.

Here is but a sampler:

- "My parents really had a hard time growing up"
- "They did the best they could"
- "They were really struggling when I was a child"
- "My Dad spent long hours at work trying to help the family survive"
- "Trying to avoid the mistakes of their own parents they swung too far the opposite way"
- "Worrying about money made them angry but they were trying to make our life a better one than they had"
- "They did not know any better"
- "They were sickly"
- "It was the culture that shaped them"
- "It will not do any good to stir this up"
- "I can cope with my parents' shortcomings"
- "In many ways he was a good father"
- "My parents didn't became Christians until later"
- "If they knew the impact of their sin on me it would destroy them"

• "It's okay because I have broad shoulders and I can carry it"

• "It's no big deal, because I am not worth it anyway!"

When we excuse an actual trespass against us we take the focus from where it belongs, with the result that we ourselves become the focal point! Thus when the EAS victim indulges in making excuses for a parent's failures the result is predictably a tragic one. In an *Alice in Wonderland* sort of way things get turned upside-down in the mind, and the wounded son or daughter ends up signing for and accepting the poor parenting as just the natural result of their own unworthiness. This "self-inflicted transference" leaves the EAS victim in the worst possible situation, where self-esteem is so diminished they will go on wallowing unless and until rescued by a divine intervention or a skilled therapist.

When we resort to *excusing* in place of *forgiving* what we are really doing is positing that the transgressor really couldn't help them self due to a reason(s) like those listed above. If they "couldn't help it" then you have got an explanation for their actions and they have a justification for how they treated you. By excusing instead of forgiving you paint yourself into a bad corner, plain and simple.

The Curse of Usefulness

For some, excusing another's trespass against them may be coupled with the thought, "Well, he or she is just a damaged person. I should try to take care of them." This seems laudable and it does confer a sense of usefulness, meaning worth. But it is entirely *extrinsic* to what's going on in your personhood. Making oneself useful can never dissolve the consequences of a parent's failure to affirm you. Nonetheless, being useful in the eyes of others has a strong attraction for the EAS sufferer, even to the extent they will choose to make being useful their "thing" in life.

This begs a story to illustrate the utter depths the curse of usefulness can reach. Shortly after I married I was busy making myself useful by fixing things around the house. I had completed a lengthy list and returned to the kitchen to ask my wife for anything else I could do. "Well," she said, "you could check the valence lights here to see if any are burned out." Hauling myself to the kitchen ceiling I reported that all was well, no bulbs burned out. "I thought so," she acknowledged, "but you were so intent on being useful I just had to come up with something." Her next line reached into my soul. "Don't you know you don't have to do things for me in order for me to keep loving you?"

Pastors take being *useful* to a whole new level; being professional burden bearers of a sort. They really don't have much choice about having to cope with other people's burdens, as it is a part of their job. Where they can get into trouble, however, is failing to have and enforce proper boundaries.[10] A pastor's "job description" (at least in their own mind) is to be the all-accepting, all-absorbing sponge that goes about mopping up pain throughout the church community. In fact pastors can be

---

[10] Using different Greek words for "burden" or "load" the Bible contrasts crushing burdens (*baros*) to be shared with the burdens (*phortion*) a person must bear themselves. Galatians 6:2, 5)

bewildered when it appears they are not allowed to help in a given situation. And when their help isn't required they may become insecure and feel they do not belong somehow. But the very same pastor can wax irritable about having to care for so many needs and may even get resentful about being put upon! Here's the nub of it: the pastor gets everyone's garbage but feels he or she cannot tell anyone, "You are the problem!" So pastors can easily slide into the practice of excusing trespasses despite the horrific consequences to their sense of worth. Not only would confronting a people issue do no good (so goes the wrong thinking) it could have catastrophic consequences. Pastor could lose whatever affirmation he has, so he doesn't rock the boat. "If I can keep the congregation reasonably happy I'll be okay. But if I confront them I'll risk losing the affirmation I have!" Conflict avoidance becomes an acceptable trade-off and it can seem like a loving thing to do, though the Bible clearly calls for speaking the truth in love (Ephesians 4:25). You can fairly readily picture the process of becoming an EAS excuse-maker when it is presented in the context of a pastor's work within the church family. Be assured, however, that the same process can creep into the lives of the principal at the neighborhood school, a doctor at the hospital, an engineer working in a team, and myriad other high functioning EAS men and women.

Trevor Walters

13

Toward Real Forgiveness

How can we bring about a transition from living a life of excuse making to an emotionally healthy one, where trespasses are calibrated and truly forgiven? For a Christian the road to take is to speak the truth in love (Ephesians 4:25). When we speak the truth we expose what is false and this lifts people up and out of distress. (The principle is universal, so one needn't be a Christian to see the overarching benefits.)

A strategy used successfully in one of my cases was to ask a father (who was excusing his own father's behavior) how he would respond to one of his children coming to him with their own inventory of his failures to affirm them. I asked if he would want his son or daughter to forgive him or to excuse him. He was pretty adamant he would want them to make the forgiveness choice. A natural progression was to follow up by asking whether he thought his own father would want to be forgiven or excused. His answer was clear again, that his father would want forgiveness, especially as his father was a deeply Christian man. At this point it was now clear the man saw the inconsistency of his logic and was open to the forgiveness choice and re-oriented to go there.

The weakness of engaging in excuse making (in place of first recognizing the depth of an injury before going about the business of forgiving it) is often revealed by the fact the excuse(s) are actually distortions of the truth. For example, in another of my cases the excuse offered for a father's lack of affirmation of his son was that the man hadn't received affirmation from his own father and therefore hadn't learned how to affirm. This excuse began to break down and fall apart when in further questioning the client recalled his father mentoring other young men. The father was capable of affirming but chose not to exercise that choice. Painful, but the boil got lanced!

Perhaps the most frequent argument offered for a parent's shortcomings amounts to this: "Well, they did the best they could." The statement is simply not true. Who amongst us can truthfully say we really did do the best we could over even just a part of our lifetime?

Still another case I had well illustrates the difference between excuse making and forgiving a father. A client described having been dropped off at Middle School by her father, just as a schoolmate was hit by another car right in front of her. The friend was lying in the street convulsing and bleeding. The now grown woman was much traumatized by this incident in her youth. She received no understanding or support from her father for this trauma. Her parents never even asked her if she was okay. Her reaction to the lack of support was to recall that her father had seen his friend run over by a tank during the Second World War. She excused him with, "Therefore of course he didn't take care of me because he didn't know how." I reversed roles on her. "Then that would mean you wouldn't be able to be empathetic to someone who witnessed a car accident, given your childhood!" She bristled a little before it sank in and she got the point: Don't excuse yourself because of your childhood, and don't expect less of your father because of his experiences.

Another excusing technique EAS sufferers utilize is to rehearse their parents' good behaviors in order to mitigate the parenting they did not provide. I liken this to telling cop who pulls you over that your speeding should be regarded as forgivable, given all the other traffic laws you obey. Police have a dim view of such chatter, so a traffic ticket is added to your good record, and yes it really does have to be paid!

I have learned that defeating excuses is just a beginning in this phase of therapy. Excuses are like Zulu warriors that immediately step up into the front rank to replace their fallen comrades.

A turning point occurs the moment a client grasps and admits the fact they have an overwhelming need to make excuses for their parent. The next step in therapy can be taken when they comprehend that one actually has a choice either to excuse or to forgive. A question like this opens the door: "So now that you know how strongly you have needed to excuse your father's behavior, what do you think you have to gain by continuing with your excuse-making?" Frequently the response is that if the parent has an excuse then their behavior is less damaging to the client. It is a way of preserving the notion that the client is worthy and capable of being loved.

The wound is deeper if one understands that their father did have a choice to love and affirm them but in fact he chose not to do so. This therapy includes cleansing and healing deep wounds like this one. It means having the client facing up to the agonizing question of "What was wrong with me for him to actually do that?" We all run from this ultimate question. We must resist the temptation to protect the person from this wound. Instead, we must invite him or her to visit the pain of rejection.

The moment of assessing the deep wound of lack of affirmation and love must be faced by speaking the truth in love. Only then can the client see that the great sin was that of parental malpractice, and not at all that he or she was un-lovable.

Please do not think that this book enables people who want to blame others (especially their parents) for their own issues in place of having to take responsibility for facing up to things. At the heart of my thesis lies the belief that, sadly, EAS sufferers take responsibility for most everything and especially their parents' parenting.

The EAS person must first accurately discern the truth of their issue(s) and identify those that belong to the Tiger. Then, once they have done so, this therapy requires the client to eschew making excuses, give up resentment and blaming, plumb the depth of his or her wounds, and knowledgably forgive those who wounded them.

A Psychiatrist's Take

These discussions of the Affirmation Inventory and the different types of forgiveness are examples of how Trevor Walters' therapy is consistent with what has been demonstrated to be effective therapy in the secular community. Any well-trained therapist, either as a psychiatrist, psychologist or pastoral counselor, has learned of different approaches to therapy.

"For decades the dominant form of therapy was psychoanalysis, a process that could take years and in which treatment was focused on dreams, childhood memories, and the ongoing relation with the therapist (transference). " [1]

Since the appearance of psychoanalysis there have been a great many behavioral scientists bringing not only new insights into the causes of behavioral problems and psychological symptoms but also new treatments. A detailed review of the authors is beyond our scope here but a few names are worth mentioning: Ivan Pavlov, B.F. Skinner, John Bowlby, Mary Ainsworth, Abraham Maslow, Carl Rogers, Albert Ellis, and Aaron Beck along with many others have contributed to the current understanding of our complicated selves.

Based on extensive research going back to the 1950s, Albert Ellis [2,3] developed a therapy approach called *Rational Emotive Behavioral Therapy*, while Beck [4] and others published research work on *Cognitive Behavioral Therapy*, which is similar. These therapies are accepted not only by the American Psychiatric Association but psychologists as well. Based on a 1982 survey of American and Canadian psychologists Albert Ellis was considered the second most influential psychotherapist in history. Carl Rogers ranked first in the survey. Sigmund Freud was ranked third. (5) Most of Trevor Walter's techniques are similar to Ellis and Beck. These therapeutic approaches are based on what is described as an A-B-C model of emotion and behavior. The A-B-C model stipulates that it is not an Activating Event (an A) by itself that causes distress but Adversity (A) plus a Belief (B) about A that leads to C, a distressing, self-defeating Consequent emotion or behavior. Thus it is the core irrational beliefs about the adversity (in our case the lack of affirmation) that cause the client distress. Furthermore, therapeutic change will occur most quickly and changes will be most pervasive when core irrational beliefs are accurately detected, actively disputed, and replaced with alternative rational core beliefs. (2)

As we follow Trevor Walters's various techniques and experiences it is clear that they all help to identify what were the details of the lack of affirmation, what are related beliefs (often irrational) about the adversity, and what self defeating emotions or behaviors have been the consequence.

Other, more recent, authors who have influenced our author should be noted. Steve de Shazer published his work on *Solution Focused Brief Therapy* (SFBT), which is goal oriented, targeting the desired outcome of therapy as a solution rather than focusing on the symptoms or issues that brought the client to therapy. Here the therapist encourages the client to imagine the future that he or she wants, and then the therapist and client collaborate on a series of steps to achieve that goal. (6) Ivan Boszmormenyi-Nagy developed what he labeled *Contextual Family Therapy*. Based on the psychodynamic model, Contextual Therapy accentuates the need for ethical principles to be an integral part of the therapeutic process. Nagy believed that trust, loyalty, and mutual support are the key elements that underlie family relationships and hold families together, and that symptoms develop when a lack of caring and liability result in a breakdown of trust in relationships. The therapist's role is to help the family work through avoided emotional conflicts and to develop a sense of fairness among family members. (7)

Our Author has also been influenced by the pioneering work of Terry Hargrave with intergenerational families and with processes in forgiveness, aging, and intensive marital therapy that move people to practice love and trustworthiness. A Professor of Marriage and Family Therapy at Fuller Seminary, Dr. Hargrave has presented nationally and internationally and is the author of many professional articles and several books, including those referenced in the footnote below.

Jim Stanley, M.D

(1) Sadock, Benjamin, and Sadock, Virginia: *Kaplan and Sadock's Comprehensive Textbook of Psychiatry*, 7th Ed. Sippincott Williams and Wilkins Publisher (2009). ISBN 978-0781768993

(2) Ellis, Albert: *Overcoming Destructive Beliefs, Feelings and Behaviors*. Prometheus Books (2001). ISBN 978-1573928793

(3) Stevan Nielson, W. Brad Johnson, Albert Ellis: *Counseling and Psychotherapy with Religious Persons*. Lawrence Erlbaum Associates, Publishers (2001). ISBN 978-1410600707

(4) Beck, Aaron; Davis, Denise; Freeman, Arthur: *Cognitive Therapy of Personality Disorders*, 3rd Ed. The Guilford Press (2014). ISBN 978-1462517923

(5) Smith, D: *Trends in Counseling and Psychotherapy*. American Psychologist (1982) 37 (7) 802-809

(6) de Shazer, Steve: *Keys to Solution in Brief Therapy*. W.W. Norton & Company (1988). ISBN 978-0393700541

(7) Boszormenyi-Nagy, Ivan: *Foundations of Contextual Therapy: Collected Papers of Ivan Boszormeny-Nagy*. Taylor & Francis (1987). ISBN 978-0876304495

(8) Hargrave, Terry; Pfitzer, Franz: Restoration Therapy: Understanding and Guiding Healing in Marriage and Family Therapy. Taylor&Francis (2011). ISBN 978-0415876261. Hargrave, Terry: The Essential Humility of Marriage: Honoring the Third Identity in Couple Therapy. Zeig, Tucker & Theisen (2000)ISBN 978-1891944369

14

Opening Up To Grief

Grief is a natural response to a loss. Grief can manifest itself in many ways with mental, emotional and even physical aspects. People grieve a variety of kinds of losses beyond the death of a loved one, such as the end of a relationship, loss of employment, or abstractions such as "what could have been." It is the latter we focus on here.

The EAS sufferer cannot be treated without grieving things that were not part of their life but should have been. Actually facing the fact that one never heard, may never ever hear their father's unconditional affirmation is the first grief. The distant second grief is for one's parents, that they never really got to know, and hence affirm, the unique child God knew before the foundation of the world (Ephesians 1:3,4) and placed in their care.

When I was thirty-five and elected to give up on ever having my Father's blessing I went through a period of grieving. Just as when my wife Julie died some twenty-eight years later (and I had questioned if I could find any meaning without her in my life) the thought of never knowing my father's pleasure in who I am just felt like too big a burden to be dragging though life. For at least six weeks I felt sad, hopeless, and heavy with loss. For me it felt as though parental affirmation was my life force and now even the hope of it had been sliced off. Was it even possible to live a life of vitality without the affirmation I had craved?

About halfway through about six weeks of grieving[11] I realized I was no longer principally lamenting my loss. My grieving had shifted radically toward my father. Empathy arose and it had to do with my father not taking pleasure in me as his son. This was a joy God had offered him and he had missed out on it. I was now grieving for him. I have seen this grief pattern numerous times. Grief has power to open up the hurting human heart to loving once more. Grief, through intense self-focus, leads us away from feeling sorry for ourselves to being able to see other people's needs. Therefore, sadness concerning my father wasn't pity or contempt; it was genuine love for him. Getting clear about my own worth enable me to focus upon and care about another's life.

---

[11] An average grief for death of a spouse is two years.

15

Yes, You *Can Go Home Again*!

You Can't Go Home Again is a novel by Thomas Wolfe about an author who depicts his home town in ways that cause residents to send him death threats. Though the book's title has become something of a folk proverb today the fact is that an EAS sufferer can and should go home again (an imagined journey of course, not an actual visit).[12]

At this point you may be wondering what possible purpose could ever be served by an imagined visit to your home of origin. The answer in a nutshell: You are carrying toxic stuff that you need to offload. Because it is not your baggage, but it belongs to your parents instead, you will need to return it to them in order to be free of it and cleansed.

But you must not go home until you are ready for the experience. Preparing for an encounter with your parents that successfully frees you of the External Affirmation Syndrome will take time and commitment.

---

[12] You may be dealing in this and other chapters with one or both of your parents, and they may be living or deceased, so please overlook my usage of the singular or plural or present and past tenses. Just make the mental adjustments needed in your own particular case.

Not So Fast

You must not go home until you are totally ready for the experience. Insights gained from Trauma Therapy[13] can apply to the parental encounter in that an unprepared person can be re-traumatized if they are led back to re-experience the traumatic event before they've grown stronger.[14]

Even when you are ready the emotional exercise will likely deplete you physically, make you feel as though you've been run over by one of those huge garbage trucks. If you think it's going to no big deal you are probably not ready for the experience. If you are hesitant about it and maybe even a little fearful you are more realistic about the struggle this will be.

Here are some signs you are **not ready** for the

---

[13] Using a variety of techniques, including talk therapy where clients gain relief through talking with a therapist, trauma therapists help to guide victims of sudden severe shock (accidents, natural disasters, gun violence, rape, etc.) to return to an emotionally healthy pre-event state.

[14] One of the signs of premature exposure to previous trauma is dissociative behavior, ranging from a relatively mild detachment from reality to more severe dissociative behaviors where the victim shuts down emotionally and is present in mind only. In the latter state one gives the impression of a monotone, flat-faced, almost robotic person. The power of the body to shut down partially or even totally is remarkable. A case in point happened to me more than 30 years ago when I was a university chaplain counseling a student about her abortion the year before. When she fell asleep in the session I assumed she was exhausted from pulling an all-nighter preparing for exams. However the next time we met she fell asleep again, just as we approached the hours leading up to the abortion. Forewarned, I lightened the emotional intensity when she began to fall asleep during a third session and she revived almost miraculously. It was a huge learning: Individuals have their own speed of doing emotional work and they cannot be rushed.

imaginary trip to return to your home of origin:

- You are not ready if somewhere in the back of your mind you are still hoping for your parents to wake up one day and affirm you.

- You are not ready if you do not have a good grasp of the particulars of your parent's failure to affirm you. This means that not only have you completed your Chapter 11 inventory but you have faced up to each and every one of the particulars.

- You are not ready if you have not begun to grieve about what a big difference in your life it would have made if your parent had affirmed you when you were growing up.

- You are not ready unless you have begun to grieve that your parents missed out on the joy they could have taken in you as their child.

- You are not ready if you haven't rehearsed in your own mind how the imaginary encounter might go and been a little troubled by the prospect.

- You are not ready if to any degree you are motivated by anger (i.e., you would rather enjoy dumping on your parents.)

You should **delay** the encounter with your parents if:

- You are not feeling strong, even quite robust.

- You are not grieving how sad the encounter will make your parents.

- You are facing anything that requires your careful attention; e.g., you are a pastor and Holy Week is around the corner, you are caught-up in wedding plans (Get married first!) or you have a deadline at work, etc.

I think you get the point. This pivotal session will require your undivided attention and it will drain you physically. You should expect your drained physical state to last awhile.

Having prayer coverage is a vital component of your "encounter session." Having intercessors at church cover it with prayer is more than expedient.[15] Take time to stop and pray yourself, for God's blessing, for clarity of discernment, for an anointed imagination. (Yes, your imagination is the gift of God, just as much as any of your other faculties.) My practice is to pray for the Holy Spirit to indwell the client's mind and fill their imagination, such that vain or untrue thoughts do not come to mind. I pray for their protection and blessing. My final prayer is for them to be able to summon the courage to let go of the crippling need of their parents' affirmation.

Appendix 1 contains **A Word To Therapists** about the imaginary trip home.

---

[15] "The prayer of a righteous person has great power as it is working." James 5:16

16

Schlepping the Stuff

You Can't Go Home Again is a novel by Thomas Wolfe about an author who depicts his home town in ways that cause residents to send him death threats. To *schlep* (Fr., Yiddish) is to lug something with the implication of a difficult journey. ("I love hiking up Camelback Mountain but it's such a schlep with a backpack!") The client is going to imagine collecting all the bad stuff that belongs to the Tiger (the parents in this case) into a couple of garbage bags. Plastic garbage bags are useful things. You will find even imaginary garbage bags to be useful for schlepping the Tiger's output back to where it belongs.

Through the Looking Glass

Let's have a look at typical responses to be expected of the parents during the imaginary family encounter:

- Anger
- Withdrawal (Alienation)
- Shaming
- Acting the Victim

Anger

Anger is often the hardest parental response with which the client must cope. Anger has great power but to our advantage it is easily identifiable as dysfunctional. So I will ask the client, "What is it about your father's anger that stops you or makes you afraid?" Sometimes the answer springs from fear; i.e., "How can he affirm me if he is angry with me?" Here the client is still clinging to the hope that one day the parent will wake up and affirm them. This is a hope "all ye who enter here" should abandon[16] before the imagined encounter!

Anger must be separated in the client's mind from the affirmation issue. To do this I dig into whether they are thinking they made the parent angry. This is a perfect opportunity to attribute behavior to the Tiger, where it belongs. A way to do it is by analogy using different players in a different situation. For example, let's say a lady goes to her pastor with a concern about his drinking and he gets mad. Would she not see that she isn't responsible for his anger? Why in the world would she accept the responsibility for the pastor "losing it"?

Withdrawal (Alienation)

The subtly chilly act of withdrawal is catastrophic to relationships. The unstated message is: "You have so offended me that I hereby alienate you, and I am cutting-off more than just my involvement with you too, because

---

[16] There are many English translations of the famous line in Dante's *Devine Comedy* about a sign posted at the entrance to hell.

this includes detaching my good wishes as well." The worst fear of an EAS sufferer is that they could lose what affirmation they do have. My therapeutic approach is to prepare them to face this their worst fear by getting them to see how they can take back some power in the relationship if they do the leaving rather than let themselves be the one abandoned.

Being shamed by a parent can inflict a grievous wound to the soul. Here the parents take an element of truth (that a child should be grateful) and *weaponize* it to their advantage:

"How can you be so ungrateful?" "After all we have done for you!" "Why can't you be like your brother (sister)?" "Who put you up to this?" "We always sacrificed for you!"

The not so subtle message is that the child should be grateful for whatever happened in the home (which is to say they should be grateful they were not affirmed)! How twisted is that? Now the parents are absolved and responsibility is transferred to the child.

A lie can control you only if you believe it. One should "doubt the friend that lies like truth!"[17] So the therapeutic coaching is to work with the very element of truth the parents have twisted. Get the client to see that the parents have simply dumped the problem onto him or her. "So you should be grateful for not receiving your father's blessing? Just why is that?" Another approach is to ask "Okay, let's take it by the numbers. Exactly what is it that

---

[17] Macbeth, Act V, Scene V

you can indeed be grateful for?" When they have named some things you pin them down: "Very well, it is good to be grateful but are you so mindlessly grateful as to accept responsibility that belongs on your parents' shoulders? Are you really going to take responsibility that belongs to the Tiger?"

Acting the Victim

Here the parents look to have been hurt. What is really going on is they have chosen the role of victim in Karpman's[18] triangle (consisting of victim, persecutor, and rescuer) that models the connection between personal *responsibility* and *power* in the destructive shifting of roles that people in conflict can play. By taking the role of the victim the parents have put pressure on the child to take up either the role of the persecutor or that of the rescuer. Given that they crave the parents' blessing the child who has not been properly coached will unthinkingly take the rescuer's role to try to make things better for the parents. This they do by accepting the garbage back or modifying the meaning of it so it isn't a problem after all.

When parents take the role of victim they are attempting to pull-off a role-reversal wherein they are the needy one (child) and their child assumes the role of caregiver (parent). So the therapeutic coaching is to ask the child: "Whose responsibility is it to be the parent

---

[18] The Drama Triangle was developed in 1968 by Stephen Karpman, M.D. to model the connection between personal responsibility and power in conflicts, and the destructive and shifting roles people can play.

here? Did God create you to be your parents' child? Did he create you to be the parent here?"

Not "covering for" the parents in this situation may cause them some pain but in reality the root of it is their shortcomings as parents, not a child's refusal to play the game.

The "In A Perfect World" Response

Should a parent be mature and courageous enough to accept the return of their own garbage, the child is given wings! They no longer have to carry the parents' sin. The proclivity to beg for affirmation will atrophy and soon die. And now they have the means to guard their cup.

Pulling Out the Thorn

Could *Aesop's Fables* have anything to do with EAS? Well, er . . . not really, but perhaps there's a message for us in his tale of *The Slave and the Lion*. A runaway slave comes upon a lion that extends its paw, revealing a wound caused by a large thorn. The slave pulls the thorn, the wound heals and the two become friends. Our takeaway is that there are things for which even a "king of the jungle" (such as yourself) requires another's help.

In Aesop's fable the wound was disabling and it was festering. Such is the case with EAS sufferers whose own thorns disable and fester. Why do one's parents leave such an indelible stamp on their child's need for affirmation?

Many of my clients have greatly-underestimated their longings for affirmation. These mostly take cover in denial or minimization; i.e., not owning up to how deeply they feel or simply glossing-over their injury.

To evaluate this dynamic in a particular case I will ask the client to gather in their imagination a group of 5 people who will judge their worth. These must be people with demonstrated gifts of intuition and discernment, so as to render the most objective of decisions. They will have known the client in a number of contexts and over a length of time.

When the client has done the mental work and has described each of the panelists to me I will ask the inevitable question: Why wasn't your father (mother) among your top five? The answer is similar to all who suffer from EAS and amounts to saying the parent(s) are not equipped to make the necessary judgments. (In a Chess game this would be *Check*).

"Then why give your parents final say in your life when you know and acknowledge they are not qualified to judge you fairly and objectively?" Should this zinger fail to ignite an "A-ha!" moment I will ask them to tell me just why the parent isn't qualified. The answers from EAS sufferers are always more or less the same: They lack godly wisdom. They do not really know me. They've made one bad decision after another. I don't like the way they have lived their life.

"Then why do you want their approval? I ask."

A pained look crosses their face.

Checkmate!

Why trust in people who are not trustworthy? It is surprising how effective a move it is to ask the client if they would consider leaving their own children with these grandparents for an extended time. (This is not a question for early in the process when clients are sodden with excuses for their parents). For years the client has placed their trust in people who have always proven unworthy of it. That these people are the client's parents is beside the point. Now the client must deliberately reclaim the misplaced trust once and for all, and depart the home of origin taking it with them.

Trevor Walters

17

New Cups for Old

Consider these, the first and the last verses of Kipling's poem *New Lamps for Old* –

> WHEN the flush of the new-born sun fell first
>   on Eden's green and gold,
> A Lying Spirit sat under the Tree and sang,
>   "New Lamps for Old!"
> And Adam waked from his mighty sleep,
>   and Eve was at his side,
> And the twain had faith in the song that they
>   heard, and knew not the Spirit lied.
>
> • • •
>
> BUT ever we look for a light that is new, and
>   ever the Spirit cries, "New Lamps for Old!"
> And we take the lamps, and – behold,
>   the Spirit lies!

The Lying Spirit has a counterfeit on earth of every godly thing. But God is always proffering a new life and joy for Adam's life and death.

Picture a beggar's cup used for begging. Maybe tin or one of those enameled steel mugs with rust peeking through chips here and there. Utilitarian. Gets the job done. But not master-crafted for royalty.

Royalty?

Absolutely!

"But you are a chosen race, a royal priesthood, a holy nation, a people for his own possession, that you may proclaim the excellencies of him who called you out of darkness into his marvelous light." (1 Peter 2:9)

The EAS person has been going through life with a beggar's cup at the ready, searching for trickles of affirmation from all and sundry. It is not a cup suited to the royal children of a spiritual royal family, where God the Father is their father too. What's missing from this picture? Could there be another cup waiting somewhere, a very beautiful cup reflecting one's worth in God's eyes?

The imagery of a beautiful cup wasn't in my toolbox originally. I came upon it accidentally from something a client said, and yet I see now that God's grace was at work revealing a new step in this therapy.

In my seminars I take an ordinary Styrofoam coffee cup and, telling of how my father put a hole in my cup whenever he deprived me of the joy of attaining the goal he set, I poke my finger into the bottom of the cup, crush it and drop it in the waste basket. This simple act speaks powerfully to EAS sufferers. They sense their own cup is inadequate and that it is *disposable*!

Styrofoam is pretty much the opposite of how God values you and me as a royal priesthood, the temple of the Holy Spirit, a chosen people, above all loved unconditionally, no longer outsiders to God but his friends.

At this stage of the journey one of my clients offered, "My real cup, the one that God had for me, is in my parents' china cabinet. It is oh-so-dusty and has lost its shine, but I can see that it is very attractive and with a little effort it will be as good as new!" I asked if she wanted to go ahead and ask her parents if they would go get the cup and give it to her. She was hesitant but agreed to ask. Moments later she possessed the precious cup! By this simple symbolic act she had named herself as lovable, unique and worthy. I would see how powerful the special cup was in her healing in the days that followed.

The imagery of a cup that God gave them serves the recovering EAS sufferer as a powerful, almost palpable reminder of their own worth in God's eyes. This new tool gave rise to a new question I ask clients when they've unloaded the garbage bags at the parents' house: "Do you know where it is? Your cup that God has for you?"

Here are some examples of people's answers:

- Peter had moved in self-perception from being an outsider to a friend of Jesus. "On my fathers belt, dangling. There it is! It's an old fashioned cup, looks quite strong, and it is pure gold. It is so different from the utilitarian one, with the corroded bottom, I've been living with."

- Susan saw her cup clearly, a beautiful china cup, very precious, to be treasured. It was clean but empty. She asked her deceased biological father for the cup. She spoke from the heart: "I know you wanted to be my daddy, and I waited and waited hoping for that too, but now it is long past the proper time so I am taking the cup of my life back. It is time for me to leave, to grow up. But you remain my dad and the few happy memories of you that I have are in that cup. So in a very real way you are always with me. But the cup of my life belongs to me. I am grown up now and Jesus is wanting to fill my cup." She had proclaimed herself a person of worth because God created and redeemed her.

- Getting the cup back can be challenging, as was the case with David who dealt with an angry father. The cup was on his father's desk, but David was afraid even of getting his father's attention. He feared his brutalizing father would throw the cup at him. He had never been able tell even his wife about these deep feelings. I suggested walking up to the desk and taking the cup as the culmination of many hours of counseling. David did just that. As a result the father sat down looking deflated. Ties that bind had been broken, as getting the cup back became part of the healing journey.

- In Megan's case the parents did not even realize the child had a cup, let alone that she had a need for them to fill it. So it was no surprise that Megan knew her real cup was not to be found at her home of origin. She thought it could be buried in her garden, where she had often felt God's presence. Within minutes she uncovered a tarnished cup with interesting scroll-like handles. I invited her to ask Jesus what he would like to put into it. Instantly, crystal clear water was cascading into the cup and cleaning away the tarnish of years of neglect. Megan was deeply moved because she had a unique cup that was so beautiful.

- Joan is another person whose cup was buried in a garden; in this case her uncle's garden. At a very young age it had dawned on Joan that her parents were broken, so she had taken her cup away for safekeeping. Her uncle was the child's sole refuge during extended times when her mother was incapable of raising her. Despite his austere bachelor lifestyle her millionaire uncle managed through his gruff demeanor to convey enough acceptance to awaken Joan's hurting heart. Charlotte Bronte could not have penned a more powerful picture of the uncle's hushed servants gliding through vast halls, a cruel cook, a big dog to be Joan's best friend, and yes the immortal secret garden. Surmising the site was more than half the battle. Her determination did the rest. The cup was dug up and it delighted Joan. How to interpret the significance of this treasure hunt? Could we say Joan had buried her heart in a safe place all those years ago, that now she was ready to dig it up and live a more vulnerable life? I can attest that is precisely what followed in the few years that remained in her life. She made every moment count as a woman on a mission to make up for lost time. She was now alive and learning to love and celebrate herself.

- In my experience, Rebecca's story is one of the most dramatic of cup rescues. She wanted her cup back but her brutal father stood in the way. She described him as six foot-four inches of muscle, a former prizefighter. Every member of the family was terrified of his anger. She thought he would kill her if she demanded her cup. (Translation: would she die if she couldn't get him to affirm her?) When the moment came she announced, eyes closed of course, "I've got my hand on the cup now!" But fear neutralized this assertive move. Next she was telling about the size and strength of his hands. Soon after that she was biting his arm. A minute later she cried that he was trying to pull her hair out. (A group of us were offering support and comfort as this unfolded.) Minutes passed. Suddenly the triumphant words, "I have the cup! I'm getting out of the house!" Despite the great drama the results had everything in common with the experiences of other clients. Rebecca had battled for her cup and taken the prize. More profoundly, I think that through this act of grasping her cup she, like all the others, had secured her autonomy and individuated.

Make a Clean Getaway

Getting out the door with the cup and without the parent's sins becomes the objective at this point. A couple of strong emotions flood the client's heart and mind in doing so. The first is a liberating sense of freedom and hope that life is going to be so very much better. This emotion is what drives the to go over-the-top (an image from trench warfare) into the face of all that the enemy (fear) can throw at them. The liberating feeling will sustain them as they leave the house. It is the second emotion that can be problematic – a sort of bereavement that now they will never ever get their parent's blessing.

We've touched this subject before but the essence is worth repeating. I will ask, maybe even tongue in cheek, "And how long are you going to wait to see if your father will change and give you his blessing?" The client's response in the form of a question is, "I don't think it will make a difference; do you think it will?" I return service with, "You are right. Get your cup and be gone!"

Better Late than Never?

Not necessarily so! Seven days before my father died at age 88 he gave his children his blessing. We were all gathered on New Year's Eve at his house for supper, knowing that lung cancer would overtake him very shortly. At the end of the meal he made an emotional speech. It was so uncharacteristic of this "stiff-upper-lip" Brit. He lost control more then once telling us that he loved us and that he was very proud of his children!

Here were the very words I had waited my whole life to hear! Sadly, I no longer needed to hear them. God and some very wonderful people had over many years done the work of filling my cup and healing me. It felt at the time as though Dad's outpouring was to satisfy his need. I don't think I resented it in any sense or felt critical of my father, just sad for him and for us as his children. So from my own experience I would say that even if you get your fathers' blessing at the end of his life, it will have come too late, not when you needed it. And so it doesn't count for very much except as a sweet memory of him.

Leave Taking

I will ask the client where they are in the house and what the parents are doing. Clients usually report they are nearing or at the door and their parents are somewhere else in the house. (In many dozens of sessions no one has ever reported their parents at the door to see them off). I ask if they are ready to open the door, to step outside, and to close it behind them. I reassure them that Jesus will be waiting just down the street so he can be the first person to put something in that wonderful new cup. I offer comfort by letting them know I certainly understand how hard this step can be – to actually step outside and to close that door on all that is left behind. I will emphasize how this is a powerful visual of the emotional and spiritual work of leaving and cleaving:

> "Therefore a man shall leave his father and his mother and hold fast to his wife." (Genesis 2:24)

Some are emboldened to leave by joy as they hold their cup in their hands for the first time. For them it's no turning back, no last look, and off they go. At the other extreme (Rebecca biting her way to freedom) the client bursts from the house to flee. Most experiences are not so dramatic nevertheless highly emotive. For example, I asked David whether he would want to say anything to his father upon leaving. Yes, he would like to tell his father he loved him! Tragically, his dad couldn't respond. As we reflected on the hardened heart David said he was ready to leave. It was a simple yet profound exit.

A Psychiatrist's Take

The use of visualization techniques to carefully walk through actual past events (adversities) is an important part of this therapy. As the author makes quite clear it is not enough just to know that there were adversities amounting to non-affirmation in one form or another, although it is the beginning place. Indeed, it is essential to gather an understanding of the individual's very specific feelings at the times these events happened, and then to see how their thought processes subsequently evolved into the various beliefs (often irrational ones) that they hold concerning these events. Retracing one's hurtful interactions with a parent(s) – on a minute-by-minute basis, as much as possible – can clarify the origin of current feelings and beliefs, as well as behaviors that may be harmful or self-defeating. Not all clients can visualize such past events with equal clarity, but the effort is justified to first understand the origin of misguided beliefs and behaviors and then to lead one to a more rational view of the past and healthier behaviors.

Jim Stanley, M.D.

Trevor Walters

18

Guarding Your Cup

At the height of a doctrinal crisis raging in my former denomination a recovering EAS victim was hauled before Sanhedrin to be brutalized by furious "Bulls of Bashan"[19] bent on the destruction of everything he affirmed and stood for. It happened. Hostility dripped from their enraged jowls. It was hellish. It was meant to disembowel him spiritually.

I know because I was the prey for their lions' teeth that day.[20] Maybe the whole thing is a story for another book but the episode is useful here: How could a former EAS sufferer, who had led a life craving approval and avoiding confrontation, rise to a challenge like this? My EAS had been crippling, and never so much as when in the presence of higher authority. I share what follows as a testimony to God's healing.

Anticipating a trial by fire, I told my wife Julie I would not need my cup that day, and I deliberately left it with her for safekeeping. These were my superior officers in the church; however, I felt empowered knowing I did not

---

[19] The Psalmists' euphemism for religious leaders (Psalm 22:12).

[20] They had turned me down on a request and feared I wouldn't abide by their decision. When all was said and done I affirmed my respect for their authority because their position didn't violate Scripture.

need affirmation from them. I decided I did not want their approval and their attacks were not going to pierce my spirit and hurt me. God gave me a vision a little while earlier that had also been a great strength. (Whether we count it as such or not most of us have had a vision at some time in our lives). In it I saw a grand fortress with many steps leading up to two large doors. On either side of the doors at the top of the stairs was a huge roaring lion. The Lord whispered in my ear, "Your job is to go up the stairs and to speak truth to the people inside. The lions are chained, so if you walk up the middle of the staircase they can't reach you."

The attack and challenge upon entering was as bad as I had expected, if not worse. I felt totally despised and rejected, but somehow it mildly amused me. I do believe I spoke the truth boldly but with love. Knowing that I needed nothing from these men carried me right up to the edge of a dangerous emboldening. I felt more sense of personal power than I had ever felt in my life. I saw their arguments mushroom and then atrophy. They sounded the retreat by fleeing for cover behind the opinions of people not present who, they assured me, thought their position was the right one! I was evicted and I left quietly. But not before I said "I think your decision stinks!" I could have used more circumspect language, but that's what happened! I had safeguarded my cup when I knew I would be disparaged. Most importantly, Jesus had topped-off my cup.

Letting Jesus Fill Your Cup

When the Father spoke at Jesus' Baptism and again at the Transfiguration Jesus was reassured about who he was and to whom he belonged, "... my beloved Son."[21] These three words meant Jesus was loved and that he belonged to the Father. The safest person you can let speak into your life is Jesus himself. He reassures us of who we are and to whom we belong. You are his loved son or daughter! You belong to Jesus! Once these two foundational facts are in place you can endure anything.

One of the great joys of my ministry is to listen in as Jesus speaks into the lives of my clients. The words they hear are always perfectly fitted to their deepest needs. One example will suffice for the many, the case of a man I shall call Peter who, imagining Jesus, burst forth with . . .

"Those understanding eyes, looking at me. Jesus knows me. He said just one word – '*Mine!*'"

Here was the highest truth there was or ever will be – you are his! You did not choose him. He chose you. What Jesus said to Peter was the perfect antidote to the poisonous words of Peter's mother, who disowned him. "Exactly!" Peter confirmed.

A final word about guarding your cup: always bear in mind the difference between interacting with so-called best friends and engaging with true peers. An EAS person

---

[21] Matthew 3:17; 17:5
Mark 1:11; 9:7
Luke 3:22

is susceptible to having superficial "best friends" who are not discerning people and will move on once they tire of the relationship. Worst of course is a tango of two needy persons. Nothing much will come of that except enduring neediness.

The characteristic I have found important in a best friend relationship is *reciprocal vulnerability*, where the friends "put out" equally in sharing themselves. Without emotional reciprocity of this kind the relationship is one-sided, without depth, and unlikely to last. Peer-to-peer relationships are more likely to endure and develop into true friendships.

Getting one's cup back results in a rethinking of who will be allowed to be in my inner circle; in particular, who will be allowed to be a best friend. Here is a guide to rethinking who that should be. Best friend relationships are based on:

- Shared common interests.
- Mutual respect. Each values the other as a person, as well as their opinions and their beliefs.
- Mutual challenge. Each challenges the other to grow and to face issues in life.
- Neither protects nor uses the other.
- They have no should-dos. Neither friend has to engage with the other, but both are free to do so whenever they choose.

Now let's see who else besides Jesus you are going to let have access to your cup.

The Blessing of Discerning People

What does it mean to be discerning? A discerning person demonstrates good perception, understanding and insight. A discerning person exhibits good judgment. In a nutshell: they have wisdom. They are the only people who should have access to your cup. It is a blessing to have one or more discerning people in your life. It is a blessing when they put something in your cup, especially when it is the truth told in love. None but the discerning should have the privilege or be allowed.

The best examples of discerning people are found in Jesus and the Apostles. We are not gifted with the Apostles in our daily lives (except in print) but we can look to them and to Jesus for modeling the wisdom that attends godly discernment.

What a wonderfully powerful moment it must have been in the lives of people Jesus affirmed. Imagine the Centurion when he was told what Jesus said about him.[22]

> "You've got to be joking! He really said that? I've got more faith than their Chief Priest?"

> "That's what he said, all right."

If that Roman soldier let those affirming words into his heart (and how could he not?) can't you see how he would seek to exemplify the man of faith that Jesus had named him? Discerning affirmation produces good fruit!

---

[22] I tell you, not even in Israel have I found such faith (Luke 7:9).

The Apostle Paul made sure to affirm his subordinates who were performing well. He began almost all his Epistles with a thanksgiving section affirming whomever he could affirm. Only then did he write about the issues of the day. Affirmation was foundational for Paul. He himself went to Jerusalem to seek affirmation from the Apostles, who were the discerning people in his own life.

> "And when James and Cephas and John, who seemed to be pillars, perceived the grace that was given to me, they gave the right hand of fellowship to Barnabas and me, that we should go to the Gentiles and they to the circumcised." (Galatians 2:9)

Paul was clearly affirmed by these pillars of the Church that day in Jerusalem, although it was to be short-lived. Later on Paul would need to guard his cup for a season when they were having difficulty adjusting to the agreement they had made with him.[23]

Paul's use of the thanksgiving affirmation in his epistles would reach new heights in his letter to the Ephesians:

> "For this reason, because I have heard of your faith in the Lord Jesus and your love toward all the saints, I do not cease to give thanks for you, remembering you in my prayers."
> (Ephesians: 1:15,16)

---

[23] Galatians 2:11-14

Paul wanted the people he was addressing to know they were really special. We can only imagine how pleased the Ephesians were for St Paul himself to see into their hearts. One hopes they let the affirmation sink in and didn't just slough it off with pseudo spiritualizing: "Oh, It wasn't us but Jesus working in us." I expect Paul would have retorted, "Look, I know that but it was your heart and your character that he used!" His letter to the Philippians contains eight versus of thanksgiving (see Philippians 1:3-11). His affirmation is deeply intimate. He "holds them in his heart." He "yearns for them with the affection of Jesus Christ." Every time he prays they come to mind as his partners and friends. Merely thinking of them makes him feel warm inside. These lovely affirmations surely filled the cups of the saints at Philippi. Being their spiritual father, Paul was the one they needed to hear from. His pleasure in them would have greatly blessed them. In Colossians 1 Epaphras is singled out in the eleven verses of thanksgiving. He receives special affirmation as a shining example of a faithful minister.

You can be sure Epaphras took that straight to the bank.

Trevor Walters

19

Drinking from Your Cup

Affirmation is not like a fine wine that need to be put away to age before it is ready to be enjoyed. Affirmation is drinkable whenever, so you should have a celebratory sip from you cup now and again and savor the moment. It will keep you going in the right direction.

- When God appointed David to be king he celebrated before the Lord. (2 Samuel 6:21)

- All the people celebrated when the temple was built in Jerusalem. (Ezra 6:16)

- The father celebrated the Prodigal's return. (Luke 15:32)

Timeouts to celebrate are health giving, both spiritually and physically:

"A joyful heart is good medicine, but a crushed spirit dries up the bones." (Proverbs 17:22)

It isn't prideful to celebrate good tidings, happy events and personal achievements. A baby's first steps, awards at school, promotions at work; all these merit a celebration. Don't you think that God takes delight in our happy milestones? He does. As David was quick to say,

> "Great is the Lord, who delights in the welfare
> of his servant!" (Psalm 35:27)

In stark contrast, no successes of mine were ever celebrated when I was growing up. Whenever the carrot was almost within reach my father would move the goal beyond reach again. He likely thought he was coaching me well and toughening me up, but it was abusive because I could never get the hang of it or see the purpose. It was hurtful and disempowering, taking even more energy when I had to get up and go after it again.

"Moving the goal post" (the old saying is of British origin) captures the unfairness of changing the rules during a game or a process.[24] Done repeatedly it will assure that an individual may not achieve their goals, and they will certainly not feel satisfied with their adequacy.

While growing up I wasn't allowed to have timeouts to celebrate successes. (Of course once the goalpost got moved there was no success). The goal that I thought would reap a reward always turned out to be just a stepping-stone to another, more distant goal. I never derived any pleasure from my achievements because none was ever regarded as a milestone – it was good work to be sure, but work that could have been even better I was given to understand.

By the Grace of God it did begin to change for me. When I completed my doctoral work some 25 years later

---

[24] A Danish goalkeeper was caught on camera literally moving the goalposts during a football game in 2009. A referee discovered it during the game but the miscreant did not suffer suspension or any fine for his action – nor did my father!

I received a few little remembrances, including a very nice mug labeled *Congratulations*! My professors deemed I had successfully completed the program and all of its requirements, and so the University conferred on me the degree Doctor of Ministry. Believe me, I "took it to the bank" emotionally! And I enjoyed drinking my morning coffee from that mug every day, savoring the taste of success in completing my academic marathon.

For a long time afterward I drank my morning coffee and daily ration of wellbeing, peace and self worth from my *Congratulations* mug. I didn't go rushing out to find the next goal. I was just basking in the celebration of my achievement. And I felt incredibly self-indulgent until slowly something very wonderful began to happen to me. Having gotten the hang of the business of celebrating, I began to celebrate successes big and small. I would treasure any affirmation given to me and reflect upon the affirming words people would put into my cup. I would try them on for size as the Centurion may have done ("You have got to be joking!"). But then I would move along to the place of, "Well, what if that were really true of me?" and I would begin to try to live into those words.

In my former life as an EAS person I discounted affirming words, even affirmations from people I new were discerning. Within hours the affirmations were vague memories or forgotten because I had turned my back on them. And so I kept on feeling unworthy. The great difference now is that my cup is full and I can and do drink affirmation from it. Not every day but often enough, having set aside enough interrupted time to make it a grace filled moment. Having my morning coffee while phoning and doing work is mindless and gives me no "coffee experience." But when I sip my coffee nestled with my wife, enjoying her company, I partake in a beautiful moment. Savoring affirmation from your cup should be in moments deliberately special like that.

Journaling is a wonderful way to catch affirmations and preserve them. They become money in the bank in years to come. Recently, at age 65, I climbed up a 30-foot telephone pole, stood upright on a 12 inch by 30 inch board affixed at the top, then leapt to a trapeze bar that seemed out of reach, in order to be lowered safely back to earth. (Oh, and there was someone already standing on that tiny board atop the pole as I strained to stand next to him! That meant the two of us would coordinate our leap toward the same trapeze bar!) Overcoming my vertigo by standing up on a tiny square of plywood toping a thirty-foot poll has leveled the playing field for me in facing other fears since. Success breeds success. It took a great deal of courage for me to risk my physical safely that way. I celebrated my courage with the Adventure Course challenge making it into my journal in a surprisingly firm hand that evening!

Sipping from the cup should not lead to pride but to an accurate appraisal of oneself. I do not want to think more highly of myself than I should. Neither do I want to dishonor the person God created by thinking any less of myself than godly discerning people have observed and confirmed. I want to know myself as God sees me. I want to reflect on how discerning people see me. I do not want to live in the imaginations of my own heart, because they can wax arrogantly or tear me down to the depths. I need to live in community. To live a life withdrawn from the opinions of other people is just as dangerous as dependency on what others think. Life in community means I receive the affirmation and counsel that is offered in love and godly discernment, and I choose to reciprocate by seeking ways that I can affirm the people around me.

A Psychiatrist's Take

To review, we know that Trevor's clients experienced significant adversities in the form of non-affirmation. We have seen that responses to the adversities represent a great variety of intense emotions, coupled together with a wide spectrum of different non-adaptive thoughts and behaviors. Through discussion and visualization a clear picture of each individual's adversities and subsequent irrational thoughts and behaviors become known. But it is not enough just to have insight about the cause of non-adaptive thoughts and behaviors.

It is extremely important to replace harmful patterns of belief and behavior by putting new ones into place to reinforce the insights gained. It is not enough just to understand about good diet and regular physical exercise; one has to apply that knowledge. The author's examples of more adaptive behaviors are sound ones; including finding and developing constructive peer relationships, cutting wasteful activities from our schedules, seeking affirmation only in healthy situations, and seeking a more intimate relationship with God.

Jim Stanley, M.D.

20

Sharing from Your Cup

We are called to be good stewards of the godly gifts we have recieved. In the Book of Genesis God told Abraham:

> "I will bless you and make your name great, so that you will be a blessing." (Genesis 12:2)

We are blessed in order that we ourselves may be a blessing to others. You are truly blessed if you have been rescued from that dreadful prison called EAS, and now the time has come for you to step into a new life characterized by confidence and humility. No, that isn't an oxymoron! You can be like Jesus. He was supremely confident and thoroughly humble. His confidence was not bravado and his humility was not self-effacement. His life was centered in the fact he was (and full-well knew he was) the Father's beloved son. My counsel in this is simple: Let your heart take courage. (Psalms 27:14; 31:24) If you are a Christian, be confident that your life is hidden with Christ in God, that you are his beloved child even now (Colossians 3:3). Step right into you new life as the wounded-healer.

Now I want to review several aspects of what sharing the blessings in your cup might look like.

131

Sharing what is in one's cup has of course a ministry dimension. An exercise I ask people to do at this stage is to review their schedule of appointments with a particular eye to identifying what I call *ministry appointments*. I have them photocopy the last few months' of their appointments and circle those meetings or phone calls where they experienced something like an inward groan or sigh about who they were going to have to encounter that day. Why were some "must-do" encounters life depleting while others were neutral or even life enriching? Why did they feel as though they had to keep some of the life depleting sessions going?

Many years ago when I was still in parish ministry I did this exercise myself and I concluded that if these encounters were life depleting for me perhaps they were for the other person as well. To my surprise the first person to whom I mentioned I felt as though I had reached the limit of how I could be of help to them shrugged. "I was wondering that too. I felt we were done a couple of sessions ago."

Inertia (the tendency to do nothing or to remain unchanged) seems to have a disproportionate effect on self-appointed burden bearers, who apparently assume that life always has to be difficult and that their job is to put their heads down and keep on slogging. I realize that life involves significant, sometimes great, self-sacrifice and is not meant to be self-centered. My words here are meant as a corrective to EAS sufferers, not to license laziness or slothfulness.

EAS people are so used to saying *yes* when someone asks for help that they don't even think about the possibility of saying *no*. Sharing *oneself* – your time, your energy and your emotional resources – needs to be based on a deliberate and responsible choice. You must first and foremost take care of your own needs and those of your marriage and family, and love your neighbor as your self, before you even think about taking on the needs of others.

EAS people often shortchange the ones they love. Family needs get sacrificed in a desperate attempt to fill one's cup with accolades for well doing, leaving the EAS sufferer depleted with little or nothing left for their children and spouse. In my first parish I was so in need of being seen to do a good job as the young curate (assisting priest) that I would come home emotionally and physically exhausted with nothing to give my wife and children. I was so afraid of rejection by the church that I sacrificed my family's need of a husband and father who was emotionally available. Looking back I see that I lived at the edges of burnout for years, driven to overwork by my EAS.

Building Healthy Relationships

In my experience chronic victims and rescuers in this life always seem to find each other. That's because each has a need the other fills. The victim is insatiably needy; the rescuer enjoys a certain sense of being in control, and of being over-adequate to make up for an inner sense of under-adequacy. This is a broad-brush way of saying that symbiotic relationships (co-dependent relationships based on need) are unhealthy. Well, you knew that of course, but what I want you to see is that in terms of emotional content healthy relationships are not need-based at all. Let me put it this way: The EAS person has been too focused on "How am I being perceived?" to think much about who they would like to have as a really good friend. Ah, but the new level of worth of the wounded-healer gives rise to a yearning for friendships where one can share reciprocally. The wounded-healer with his or her cup now full wants to find and relate personally with other people whose cups are also full, while on another level they will respond to those whose cups are empty as one beggar giving another wine.

One no longer has room for need-based relationships that lack mutuality in the area of sharing. In searching for new good friends the question to ask is "Who do I know that I really respect?" Such a person isn't emotionally needy. Another question to ask oneself is "What are the qualities I want to see in a good friend?"

Having identified a person or persons who seem to meet your criteria, your next step is to begin a non-manipulative, well, a sort of a "dance" with them. Reciprocal openness to one another is the key to sharing in healthy relationships. Giving a little of yourself and seeing if the other person matches your depth of disclosure is the means of finding out if the relationship is going to be a balanced one. (Here is a good place to pause to review the qualities of a discerning person that we covered in Chapter 18 at pages 121-123.)

21

Parenting Yourself

The upshot of your journey from EAS sufferer to being healed of EAS is that you have seized the parental role from your parents, so that from now on you are going to be parenting yourself!

Selah![25]

It is important to internalize and accept your new role, and get to work on becoming a loving parent of yourself. I say work because parenting is challenging and you will be doing it for the rest of your life.

Good parenting skills are second nature to anyone who experienced loving affirmation as a child. These people have good memories of being well parented in a multiplicity of situations, and they do likewise almost instinctively. Not so with "a little sponge" whose parent had a critical spirit or was given to impatience or anger or other poor behavior. Their memory bank must be re-written by a new loving parent, a process that may take a long time.

---

[25] The meaning of *Selah* (a word used more than 70 times in Psalms) is unknown, but some scholars think it was meant to impart something like, "Take a minute to let that really sink-in!"

You yourself are that new loving parent! What kind of parent will you be?

- Will you have realistic expectations [26]
- Will you be a demanding parent?
- Will you be a critical parent?
- Well you engage in recriminations?
- Will you shame yourself?
- Will you be an encourager when you fail?
- Will you encourage humility?
- Will you permit self worth to flourish?
- Will you always affirm yourself?
- Will you allow yourself to celebrate?

A Psychiatrist's Take
Summation

Trevor Walters' concepts and techniques are compatible with mainstream practice of the American Psychiatric Association, with some minor exceptions. His

---

[26] Having realistic expectations in life is preventative medicine and an antidote to depression and discouragement. I know from what little golf I play that unrealistic expectations of playing a better round will cause my game to go even further awry.

proposed diagnosis of External Affirmation Syndrome (EAS) is not in the DSM-V but that does not imply an incompatibility. The mental disorders in DSM-V are virtually all defined by published research data from multiple academic institutions and based on patients who have been treated in medical settings. So when a well trained, highly experienced pastoral counselor/author like Trevor Walters sees a definite pattern of symptoms in a number of his cases, and finds it useful to put a label on it for his colleagues and clients, then I believe it is a significant contribution. Regarding the techniques for helping his clients, all of his procedures in my opinion are compatible with current psychiatric treatment. The treatment orientation of the author fits DSM-V except for the biological component. His techniques are widely accepted and are not practices that to be skeptical about.

As stated at the outset clear issue that distinguishes this book from secular academic psychiatry is the theological component – the author grounds the issue of blessings and affirmation in theology. This means that he and his clients believe in the divine healing power of Jesus Christ. Before the counseling described here can begin the counselor and client must agree on this issue, but otherwise the process presented in this book is consistent with mainstream psychiatry.

The author uses two main therapeutic techniques in treating the symptoms of External Affirmation Syndrome: These are *psychodynamic psychotherapy* and *cognitive-behavioral* therapy. Both are widely accepted in the broad psychological and psychiatric communities. Psychodynamic psychotherapy is used to help the patient understand the connection between parent-child relationships and their current feelings and beliefs. Using cognitive-behavioral therapy the patient is directed to focus on certain beliefs and behaviors and to consider whether these beliefs and behaviors are rational.

Visualization of past experiences as employed by the author can help the patient understand where inappropriate attitudes, behavioral patterns, and negative feelings may have originated. The understanding gained in this way can serve to help the patient modify irrational beliefs and behaviors. The author's discussions of an "affirmation inventory" and different types of forgiveness demonstrate that his therapy is consistent with what has been demonstrated to be effective therapy in the secular community.

Most of the techniques discussed in this book are similar to those of the landmark researchers Albert Ellis and Aaron Beck. These therapies are accepted by the American Psychiatric Association and in the field of psychology as well. Trevor Walters' work also shows some influence from recent pioneers in therapies that are not dissimilar from his approach. These include Steve de Shazer's work on *Solution Focused Brief Therapy* (SFBT), Boszmormenyi-Nagy's work on *Contextual Family Therapy*, and Terry Hargrave's work on processes that move people to practice love and trustworthiness.

Most importantly Trevor Walters has shown us how extremely important it is to replace harmful patterns of belief and behavior by putting into place new healthy ones that reinforce the insights gained from this therapy.

His examples of adaptive healthy behaviors are sound ones.

Jim Stanley, M.D.

A Final Note to the Reader

Although this book is about burnout in persons lacking parental affirmation, I feel that something ought to be said about how to affirm one's children. I asked my dear friend The Rev. Terry Lamb to write it for me, because I have known him to be a most godly father to his children, who are now grown with children of their own. Appendix 3 contains his wisdom on the subject. I commend it most highly. Appendix 4 is a list of some Healing Ministries known to me or to my editors. I'm sure there may be many other goods ones that may be closer to your home.

Trevor Walters

About the Author

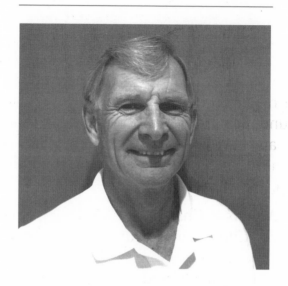

Bishop Trevor Walters

Trevor Walters is perhaps best known as a therapist for his decades of work with burned out clergy. He holds a Doctor of Ministry degree form the University of Edmonton, where he has served on the Master's of Theology Council. He has had the high honor of serving the University of Calgary as University Chaplain.

London born, the author was ordained at Salisbury Cathedral and sent to Canada to serve as curate at a parish in Calgary. He was Rector at St. Matthew's Church in Abbotsford, Canada, Anglican Church of Canada, until resigning in defense of Biblical orthodoxy. He is now Bishop of Western Canada for the Anglican Network in

Canada, a part of the Anglican Church in North America. Earlier in life he taught high school in England, having qualified at London University. He came to know the Lord at age 15, attended a Baptist Church, and was mentored by a Plymouth Brethren teacher. Later he joined the Barnabas Fellowship, an early charismatic community in England, where he learned to pray for people in depth and was taught by inspirational leaders from around the world. His seminary training was at Salisbury and Wells Theological College, an Anglo-Catholic institution, due to its relationship to Barnabas Fellowship.

Bishop Walters is Chair of the Mediating Committee of the Anglican Church in North America, and a Circuit Civil Mediator for the Supreme Court of Florida. Most recently he has functioned variously as a counselor, mediator, preacher, lecturer, and as a Bishop, in Canada, Cuba, Sudan, the UK and the United States.

Julie, Trevor's wife of 30 years, died after decades' long battles with life threatening illnesses. After some years of loneliness he was surprised by the joy of meeting and marrying Dede Johnson, and they now share the life of faith and their six children and four grandchildren. As Trevor says, "God has brought me great life in the midst of death, great joy in the face of overwhelming loss, and deep love in the midst of aloneness." Trevor Walters is an avid hiker, kayaker, and golfer. He thrives on challenge.

About the Psychiatrist

Ernest James (Jim) Stanley, M.D.

Dr. Stanley was educated at Stanford University and the Yale School of Medicine. His education in psychiatry was furthered at the University of Munich, Germany, Stanford Hospital, and the University of Colorado Medical Center.

Dr. Stanley is a member of the American Psychiatric Association and a Diplomate of the American Board of Psychiatry and Neurology. He is retired following 30 years of the private practice of psychiatry in Newport Beach, California. Dr. Stanley has served as psychiatric consultant to a variety of mental health programs in

Colorado and California, including more than 15 years as Director of Student Mental Health Services at Orange Coast College. Earlier he was a psychiatrist in the United States Air Force Medical Corps, with the rank of major. Dr. Stanley is the author or co-author of several published works including *Overcoming Obesity in Adolescents* [Clinical Pediatrics, 9-29-36] and *Adolescent Suicidal Behavior*, Am. J. Orthopsychiatry 40:87-96].

Jim Stanley and his wife Rhoda are the parents of three grown children and have eight grandchildren. They enjoy golf and bridge, and especially time with their kids and grandkids. Jim and Rhoda Stanley attend St. Andrews Presbyterian Church in Newport Beach, California.

Acknowledgements

First and foremost, to my wife Dede who has affirmed and encouraged me. She believes in me and her wise counsel continues to watch over my risk-taking propensity. Dede's love forever heals my heart. Her discernment causes me to draw rapid breath! How sweet to do life together.

To Ron Speers who has been a champion of my work. His enormous dedication to this project has deeply moved me. In the event of the Editor becoming ill, Ron went a second mile, beyond the bounds of Publisher, taking on the role of the editor too. Ron has become a good friend and a mentor. He also introduced his good friend psychiatrist Jim Stanley to this project. I am deeply indebted to Dr. Jim's authoritative yet deeply personal voice that has spoken over my work. To Kathryn Bardolph – a professional editor – who nearly missed her European vacation to provide a last minute second eye to the work. One gifted and gracious lady! To Bud Davis whose meticulous touch improved the manuscript.

To my children without whom this would never have been written. Sarah, Mark and Tim, you amaze me and I am so proud of you and your families! To my stepchildren Anna, Krista and Eric, you are awesome!

Thank you all from the bottom of my heart,

Trevor

Trevor Walters

Appendix 1

A Word to Therapists About the Imaginary Trip Home

The purpose of this exercise needs to be made crystal clear to clients: (1) they have to leave the garbage bags with their parents, naming the contents as not belonging to themselves; (2) They need to leave the house knowing that they will never again return as an affirmation-seeking You must ensure that the client is ready, and that their physical and emotional energy is strong. This must be a separate session (or more than one session). The parental encounter is never a good idea as part of a regular counseling session.

Preparedness is vital. Visualizing some scenarios of what might happen in the encounter and how the client might cope is essential. This work is to be done in previous sessions, never on the day of the great encounter.

You will employ the respected Action / Reflection procedure.[27]

---

[27] Dear Reader: This may sound like professional hocus-pocus but it isn't, nor is it just looking back on past happenings *per se*. This therapy involves being helped to deliberately unpack actions, responses, and emotions in order to gain clarity about them, and thus reach a higher level of understanding about one's personhood in a non-threatening way. "Reflection is an important human activity in which people recapture their experience, think about it, mull it over

I think these points are important ones:

- Do not get into unnecessary chatter about the encounter session beforehand. Have the big encounter first and talk about it afterwards.

- To begin the session I announce that we are both going to close our eyes and keep them closed throughout. (That my eyes are closed too is liberating for the client.)

- I tell the client my function is to coach them along and offer feedback as may be helpful, so I will be interjecting occasionally.

- If there was more than one family home while the client lived with their parents I will ask them to identify which house they have chosen. (I am interested in exactly the stage in their life where strong and or troubled memories are triggered.)

- I tell the client they must keep-on-keeping-on as they give me a running commentary, so I can follow along with where they are in the house and what is happening.

- When the client has pictured arriving at the house I ask how they are feeling about ringing the doorbell or knocking in the old familiar way. (I want to establish how present they are to their emotions, so as to rule out a mind-only exercise in a dissociative

---

and evaluate it. It is this working with experience that is important in learning." Boud, David; Keogh, Rosemary; Walker, David (1985). *Reflection, turning experience into learning*. London; New York: Kogan Page; Nichols. p. 19. ISBN 0893972029.

state). Asking what they smell or can hear while standing at the front door is another way of establishing they are engaged emotionally and not making it up. If I sense they are play-acting and not really into it emotionally then we will not go into the house today but we will be spending more time on preparation in our next session.

- If I sense at any point in the encounter that they are apprehensive or fearful I will ask how they are feeling and offer encouragement.

- When silence ensures I want to judge if it is a useful pause or if things are at an impasse. However, I do not want to risk drawing them out of the encounter just because they are overly aware of my presence. So I am mostly quiet, only asking a question or making a comment when necessary to keep things moving along.

- When I sense things are not moving forward I will ask where they are in the house and what is happening. I might also try to connect them to their senses; smell for example, by asking if they detect any odors in the house. Scents are more distinct in memories of long ago than are feelings. (One of my clients was quick to report the waft of cigar smoke and culinary smells just as soon as he was inside the house).

- Some people are relaxed and almost chatty in blow-by-blow reporting. Others struggle being able to verbalize and need more encouragement and Q&A in order to share freely.

- One of my functions is to reflect on their behavior to see if they are acting in such a way as to keep their parents happy with them. This would indicate that their need of parental approval is still a driving force in their life. When I see this type of behavior I'll ask if they are saying this or acting that way in order to keep their parents happy. (Clients seldom bristle at this but typically will nod or smile in recognition of how deeply ingrained their EAS really is.)

- I am particularly interested in where they find their parents in the house. I will want to know how they were greeted.

- I will want the parents' reaction to garbage bags being offloaded at their house.

Appendix 2

Lists In This Book

The lists in this book are reprinted here for quick reference and ease of copying:

Observable Symptoms of Burnout

STAGE 1

- Insomnia / Broken sleep patterns
- Weakened immune system
- Restlessness / Loss of peace
- Loss of a vision / Disappointed in life
- Not participating in daily activities that used to delight / Loss of joy
- Fatigue
- Irritability / Fruits of the Spirit diminishing
- Frustration
- Inward criticism expressed as negative self talk
- Difficulty concentrating
- Running on adrenaline
- Swearing under breath
- Diminished impulse control
- Anxiety
- Seeking comfort in destructive ways: over-eating, pornography, fantasy, etc.
- Defensiveness
- Difficulty trusting other people
- Confusion
- Conflicted
- Avoidance / Putting off dealing with issues
- Digestive tract disturbances / Stomach problems

- Everything depends on me / I carry the weight of the world
- Feeling useless

STAGE 2

- Anger outbursts or anger at self
- Looking for or dreaming of another position as a way out.
- Critical of others
- Feeling hurt, let down, neglected, even overlooked by God
- Complaining
- Insomnia making daily functioning more difficult
- Bursts of adrenalin followed by crashes
- Changed work habits / Overworking and or working less efficiently
- Memory lapses, e.g., losing keys, forgetting previously known details
- Exhausted / Worn out
- Depressed
- Heart hardening towards God

STAGE 3

- Acute fear with likelihood of panic attacks
- Social phobia
- Paranoia
- Isolation
- Alienation of friends and allies

- Acute sensitivity to stimuli; i.e., sounds, sights, touch, smell
- Drastic reduction in physical ability and stamina
- Heart hardened towards God and others
- Too exhausted to be angry
- Spouse increasingly the brunt of the anger
- Easily moved to tears
- Acceptance of the need for extended time off

In my opinion, the presence of 50% or more of these observable symptoms is suspicious for a diagnosis of burnout. It should be noted that this inventory overlaps a diagnosis of depression or post-traumatic stress disorder (PTSD). If a person also checks off more than 50% of the Affirmation Inventory (pages 161-162), then treatment of burnout caused by EAS is preferred.

Symptoms of EAS

- Conflict avoidance
- Feelings of unworthiness
- Feeling of inferiority
- Feelings of not belonging in groups
- Undue subjectivity
- Obsessive need for approval
- Confusion when affirmation is given
- Discounting affirmation when given
- Approval evaporating quickly
- People-pleasing
- Not having a regular day off
- Perfectionism and overworking
- Being critical of others' work habits
- Resentment at not being appreciated
- Exhaustion / Flirting with burnout
- Anxiety
- Insecurity

Sharing One's Cup

The non-addictive person keeps their cup from view, displaying it cautiously – and only when three (3) factors are well aligned:

- When they themselves have discerned that another has good discernment;[28]
- When the other person knows them well enough to be able to make a constructive judgment; and
- When the trusted person speaks with *grace* as well as truth.

Two out of the three above doesn't cut it.

---

[28] A person has discernment if they have insight into things and good judgment; in other words objectivity and common sense.

Main Behaviors of EAS

- EAS sufferers are unaware that habitually seeking after affirmation is pulling them along the path toward a midlife burnout (emotional and mental exhaustion).

- EAS sufferers are prone to *subjectivity*: their reactions to daily happenings, perceptions, beliefs and emotions are focused inwardly, inside their own minds. They have become preoccupied with how others view them and can take even trivial happenings personally.

- EAS sufferers are conflict-averse. They habitually avoid conflict in order to preserve the opportunity to obtain some affirmation. They tend to become chronic people-pleasers.

- People who do not have their father's blessing settle for their own worth as measured by *performance*.

- Thinking that more and better work will bring affirmation the EAS sufferer becomes a workaholic perfectionist who doesn't practice regular "Sabbath" days off from work.

- Failing to garner the affirmation they feel is due them, EAS sufferers will experience insecurity and anxiety and manifest anger and resentment.

Milestones in EAS Therapy

- Assessment of what the parents did about their responsibility to fill their child's cup
- Compiling a list of offences against the client
- Forgiving versus excusing the parents
- Assigning offences to the rightful person
- Taking charge of one's cup
- Leaving the home of origin with one's rightful cup
- Letting Jesus fill the cup
- Letting others fill the cup
- Drinking from the cup
- Sharing the contents of the cup with others
- Parenting one's self

Misapprehending the 5th Commandment

Clients who are sensitive to the commandment to "Honor your father and your mother," but misapprehend it to their own harm, can respond in these ways:

- They will focus mainly on the good aspects of the parenting, with a small detour to the subject of their parents' shortcomings – then and there followed up by making excuses for them.

- Some will speak at length about their parents' poor parenting, followed by a non-sequitur declaration that they were quite good parents.

- Those more aware of the underlying need to honor their parents will often say (after listing negative experiences in childhood) that they feel very bad about sharing these things. They may conclude with something like "Please don't hate my parents or think badly of them."

- Fewer will say, "I feel as though I am dishonoring my parents," but then proceed to speak openly and honestly about their parents' shortcomings.

Clarifying The Fifth Commandment

- Often a question or two works to loosen the grip of muddled thinking.

- Invite consideration of the "Covenant Expectations" of parents and children found in the Bible.

- Invite examination of how Jesus interacted with children.

- Dispel the notion of one's carrying a "bad gene."

- Maybe take a side step; i.e., get the client to view things through another's eyes.

External Affirmation Inventory

About the Affirmation

- In what ways was affirmation withheld?

- Was affirmation delayed?

- Was affirmation sometimes given but negated later?

- Was the client affirmed for achievements or for character and attitudes?

- Were comparisons made between the client and their sibling(s)?

- Was affirmation earned or was it freely given?

- How did not getting affirmation wound the client?

About the Parents

- How was the client made to feel special?

- How was the client "celebrated" (e.g., especially on birthdays)?

- In what ways were the client ignored as a child?

- Did the parents affirm others, children or adults, either within or outside the family, more than the client?

- Did the parents usurp the client's affirmation for their own benefit; for example, by telling

161

friends or neighbors about the client's successes but not telling the client?

- What did the parents put in the client's cup?
- Did the parents puncture the cup?
- Were the parents capable of giving affirmation?

About the Client

- How did the client determine that their parents loved them?
- Do they feel as though they know their parents affirmed them or are they still waiting for it?
- Do they think they are ever going to hear that they are beloved by their parents and that the parents are well pleased with their son or daughter?
- Does the client wear their cup on their sleeve, looking for affirmation from all and sundry?
- Is the client driven to succeed in order to get people's recognition and respect?
- In what ways is the client carrying too much responsibility on their shoulders?

Excusing Parental Malpractice

In my long practice I have heard a multiplicity of excuses offered for parental malpractice. Here are some of them (from page 80):

- My parents really had a hard time growing up.
- They did the best they could.
- They were really struggling when I was a child.
- My Dad spent long hours at work trying to help the family survive.
- Trying to avoid the mistakes of their own parents they swung too far the opposite way.
- Worrying about money made them angry but they were trying to make our life a better than they had.
- They did not know any better.
- They were sickly.
- It was the culture that shaped them.
- It will not do any good to stir this up.
- I can cope with my parents' shortcomings.
- In many ways he was a good father.
- My parents didn't become Christians until later.
- If they knew the impact of their sin on me it would destroy them.
- It's okay. I have broad shoulders and I can carry it.

- It's no big deal, because I am not worth it anyway!

Client Readiness to Go Home

- The client is not ready if somewhere in the back of their mind they are still hoping for their parents to wake up one day and affirm them.

- They are not ready if they do not have a good grasp of the particulars of their parent's failure to affirm them. This means that not only has the client completed their Chapter 11 inventory but that they have faced up to each and every one of the particulars.

- They are not ready if they have not begun to grieve about what a big difference in their life it would have made if their parent had affirmed them when they were growing up.

- They are not ready unless they have begun to grieve that their parents missed out on the joy they could have taken in their child.

- They are not ready if they haven't rehearsed in their own mind how the imaginary encounter might go, and been a little troubled at the prospect.

- They are not ready if to any degree they are motivated by anger (i.e., they would rather enjoy dumping on their parents.)

A client should delay the encounter with their parents if:

- The client is not feeling strong, even quite robust.

- They are not grieving how sad the encounter will make the parents.

- They are facing anything that requires their careful attention; e.g., they are a pastor and Holy Week is around the corner, they are caught-up in wedding plans, or they have a deadline at work, etc.

A Word to Therapists
<u>About Going Home</u>

I think these points are important ones:

- Do not get into unnecessary chatter about the parental encounter session beforehand. Have the big encounter first and talk about it afterwards.

- To begin the session you announce that you are both going to close your eyes and keep them closed throughout. (That your eyes are closed too is liberating for the client.)

- Tell the client your function is to coach them along and offer feedback as may be helpful, so you will be interjecting occasionally.

- If there was more than one family home while they lived with their parents you will ask them to identify which house they have chosen. (You are interested in exactly the stage in their life where strong and or troubled memories are triggered.)

- Tell the client they must keep-on-keeping-on as they give you a running commentary, so you can follow along with where they are in the house and what is happening.

- When they have pictured arriving at the house you will ask how they are feeling about ringing the doorbell or knocking in the old familiar way. (You want to establish how present they are to their emotions, so as to rule out a mind-only exercise in a dissociative state). Asking what they smell or can hear while standing at the front door is another way of establishing that they are engaged emotionally and not making it up. If you sense the client is play-acting and not really into it emotionally then they will not go into the house today but you will be spending more time on preparation in your next session.

- If you sense at any point in the encounter that the client is apprehensive or fearful you will ask how they are feeling and offer encouragement.

- When silence ensures you want to judge if it is a useful pause or if things are at an impasse. However, you do not want to risk drawing the client out of the encounter just because they are overly aware of your presence. So you will be mostly quiet, only asking a question or making a comment when necessary to keep things moving along.

- When you sense things are not moving forward you will ask the client where they are in the house and what is happening. You might also try to connect them to their senses; their sense of smell for example, by asking if they detect any odors in the house. Scents are more distinct in memories of long ago than are feelings. (One of my clients was quick to report the waft of cigar smoke and culinary smells just as soon as he was inside the house.)

- Some people are relaxed and almost chatty in blow-by-blow reporting. Others struggle being able to verbalize and need more encouragement and Q&A in order to share freely.

- One of your functions is to reflect on the client's behavior to see if they are acting in such a way as to keep their parents happy with them. This would indicate that their need of parental approval is still a driving force in their life. When you see this type of behavior you will ask if they are saying this or acting that way in order to keep their parents happy. (Clients seldom bristle at this but typically will nod or smile in recognition of how deeply ingrained their EAS really is.)

- You are particularly interested in where they find their parents in the house. You will want to know how they were greeted.

- You will want to know the parents' reaction to garbage bags being offloaded at their house.

Typical Parental Responses
<u>to the Imaginary Encounter</u>

- Anger
- Withdrawal (Alienation)
- Shaming
- Acting the Victim

<u>Best Friend Relationships</u>

Best friend relationships are based on:

- Shared common interests.

- Mutual respect. Each values the other as a person, as well as their opinions and their beliefs.

- Mutual challenge. Each challenges the other to grow and to face issues in life.

- Neither protects nor uses the other.

- They have no should-do-s. Neither friend has to engage with the other, but both are free to do so whenever they choose.

Parenting One's Self

Having seized the role from their parents, the former EAS sufferer will become their own parent now. What kind of parent will they be?

- Will they have realistic expectations?
- Will they be a demanding parent?
- Will they be a critical parent?
- Will they engage in recriminations?
- Will they shame themselves?
- Will they be an encourager when they fail?
- Will they encourage humility?
- Will they permit self worth to flourish?
- Will they always affirm themselves?
- Will they allow themselves to celebrate?

Affirmation Summation

- Affirmation is about learning the art of peace making. It speaks peace in the face of turbulence.

- Affirmation is about movement. It does not take a passive stance but looks for opportunities to connect at a deeper level with one's children.

- Affirmation is about clearing lies out of children's lives. When they think the world is caving in around them, and they are in danger of losing their way, we speak truth to dispel the lies.

- Affirmation is about patience. Affirmation waits for the right time, and the right opportunity, and the right words and the right moment – and this may even take weeks or sometimes longer.

Appendix 3

Dear Reader, it didn't seem right to close without a word on the how-to-do-it of giving children the life giving affirmation they seek, need, and deserve in order to develop as emotional healthy adults. Because my own record as a father doesn't much qualify me to write such a *coda* to this book, I asked my very dear friend and brother priest The Rev. Terry Lamb to set down his thoughts on the subject; thoughts from the parenting that he himself received and from having parented his own grown children.

I offer Terry Lamb's keen insights here, with much gratitude to him.

Dear Trevor,

When you asked me to write something on the affirmation of children I admit a part of me hoped the whole idea would just go away, not because I couldn't write about it but because of the interior journey I would need to undertake in order to make it happen truthfully.

As we age we tend to varnish over pain, the hurts, the failures and I suppose even our successes. True writing requires true confession, and that's way down deep and can be painful to unearth.

Family

Ruth and I have been married 35 years. We have six children – three daughters and three sons. It isn't a small family or a huge one, though in recent years it has expanded through marriages and births. There are now two sons-in-law, two daughters-in-law, and grandchildren – two so far.

Fourteen lives were represented around our table at Thanksgiving. There is always a lively discussion seasoned with intensity, occasionally tears, and of course laughter. There is rarely sarcasm or someone as the brunt of another's joke (though we do have a clown-prince in one of our sons, who gets it from his mother). What I observed this last Thanksgiving was that rarely was there anything like unanimous agreement, and yet everyone was fine with that!

Ruth and I had wanted to influence and shape our children to be individuals who would go on a lifelong pilgrimage to deeply discover God, the world, and themselves. Some of our affirmation was intentional and of course some of it was more accidental. To get ready to write this for you, I asked our family the simple question "How did we affirm you?" The essence of the answers comes later but first I want to begin with my own affirmation story.

It Really *Is* About The Father

I grew up in an unsafe environment. My father was a closet alcoholic, the son of an alcoholic father. Mother's father was an abusive alcoholic. My fate as a child was more or less sealed by the continuous train wreck of emotional ups and downs that I would have to endure until I left home. Or so I thought. (A child's only choice in like circumstances is escape, either physically or emotionally. I became a Houdini at both.) No one ever told me healing was an option or that my image of God the Father could be re-scripted in my life. Then I discovered that for me Jesus would be all about re-scripting the Father.

Jesus cast his Luke 15 parables (Lost Sheep / Lost Coin / Lost Son) in a language that everyone understands: Economics. One could live with the economics of a single sheep missing from a flock of one hundred. The lost coin hits closer to home, as one coin missing from ten should get anyone's attention! But the economics of the Prodigal Son are impossible to live with. A 50% loss, one of only two sons! Now Jesus really has everyone's attention! Parables target the soul and heart to re-script what has been scripted there by upbringing, life experiences, and choices. Jesus waits until the question for everyone is "Why would you give everything back to this loser without even the slightest penalty?" Then he re-scripts the Father for us, namely, what kind of God the Father is:

> *You cannot separate yourself from God!*
> *You belong to the Father!*

You can always have a place at his table.

One could summarize the message of the Old Testament prophets with one phrase: *Return to me*, as with the Prodigal. In the New Testament the first word of The Lord's Prayer is Father (*pater*), meaning the one who imparts life. The goal of affirmation is to impart life.

Consistency

Affirmation can be present in the simple matter of consistency, by being steadfast. Consistency is the first step in affirming children and cultivating a healthy environment where everyone reaches his or her potential. If you want to ruin a child, just change everyday. Wake up one morning angry, the next sad, the next happy – and it won't take you too long to ruin your children. They will not know what to expect. They will tune out. And soon enough you will have lost the opportunity to be the important influence in your children's lives and lost the battle for healthy dialogue.

Parenting happens everyday, many times over, and over and over again. We long for health in our children but often the battleground is our own spiritual and emotional health, due to our own upbringings and weaknesses. I would encourage parents to work on becoming and staying healthy themselves, emotionally, mentally and spiritually. Again, there's good reason for the little sign in airliners telling you to attend to your own oxygen mask before affixing your child's.

Affirm Personhood, Not Achievements

When we attempt to do something new or unfamiliar we are usually not very good at it at first. In the world of affirming children the rookie parent will tend to praise achievement and sort of frown on failures, instead of offering kudos for making the try at something. If that becomes the norm in the household the children will crave approval and look elsewhere for recognition their whole long lives. They will never grow into being their parents' friends, peers or advisers.

Affirmation is all about encouraging the *person* inside the child. Parents must learn to always encourage the little or young *person* in their successes or failures, and not be given to caring much about performance results.

No Room for Shame

As a priest I have learned over time that the shame of sin is more insidious than the sin itself. Shame is what makes us want to hide from God, not that we could (Genesis 3:9). Shame keeps us from becoming healthy individuals. Shame is the replay button of the soul – it replays the ugly past and keeps us at a distance from real intimacy with God, our own true selves, and others. Confession requires us to be vulnerable. Our relationships are only as deep as our vulnerability permits. But shame keeps us from confession and brings a poison to relationships. Parents must remember that shame is very toxic to a child's or a young person's dignity, while affirmation is life-giving tonic to their dignity.

Gaining Control; Giving-up Control

Ruth and I wanted our children to discover their own identities. The process to accomplish this involved gaining parental control, then giving it up *incrementally*. Control began with "Don't run into the traffic! Brush your teeth!" and so on. The object of course was to inculcate self-control so that due care would be exercised and schoolwork done without parental prompting.

It is important to let go a little bit here and there even during this stage so that the kids' identities are not stilted. How to do this carefully so the wheels don't come off the family wagon is of the utmost importance. It becomes a game of push-and-pull, and engaging the son or daughter in the push-and-pull is critical. You gently push here and pull there while young person is doing the same with you. Over time you let them gain this and you give up your control of that – but always and only when and where you can do so responsibly. You resist the strong temptation to throw up your hands in frustration and yell at a teenager, "Fine! Have it your own way." You remember that the battle is not about a "certain way" because camouflaged just under the surface is the actual battle, the battle for the kid's identity.

The struggle is about identifying and affirming the traits that make your son *him* or that make your daughter *her*. Affirming these traits helps to form the person's identity.

Your child or teen needs to know they are valued for who they are as a person. "I think you could do anything or be anyone. Can we walk through this together? I'll always be there for you!" The ultimate goal in progressing from parental control to self-control, and beyond, is progression toward God and it might sound something like this:

God, my life is yours.
What would you have of me?

Now the Father in Heaven is invited to speak life into the identity that he has for them.

Values

What we proclaim with our mouths and how we actually live out our lives will determine our success as parents. If there is a disparity between these values we will lack an anointing to affirm our children. If we say we love them but never have time for our children, our actions will be decoded long before our words, which will soon enough be discovered to be hollow. The role of parenting is both announcing that you are the parent *and* living up to the role.

Fruitage

News came to me that one of my sons failed bible class at school, and needed a talking. The son in question had enough brains to easily pass the course. Bible class was not the problem by any stretch. Failing the course was his message to his teacher and the particular institution, which lacked any spiritual depth and was more about the practice of religion than true religion itself.

Something was stirring in him and we needed to discern what it was. It came across as him telegraphing, "I don't value what you value." (He was in the push-pull teen identity-seeking time mentioned above.) A confrontation would have induced guilt and my efforts to affirm would not have been ingested. I wrestled with my response but finally went to his room, gave him a high five and said, "Well, if there is a course to fail I guess this is the one, but if you ask me I think you already passed Bible by the way you live. You're generous, you're kind and you're always looking out for others – yup, you've passed!" This caught him off guard and he didn't say much.

Two weeks later when we were driving together he asked me this, "Dad, if you really wanted to give me some advice, what would you say to me?" I answered him this way, "Son, I would not waste any energy on being cool. I would spend my life discovering God." Our talk ended with him saying, "Dad I'm coming back to you!"

Affirmation won a battle for my son. At present he is finishing up his Master's degree in theology. More importantly, he is one of my closest friends.

Summation

- Affirmation is about learning the art of peace making. It speaks peace in the face of turbulence.

- Affirmation is about movement. It does not take a passive stance but looks for opportunities to connect at a deeper level with one's children.

- Affirmation is about clearing lies out of our children's lives. When they think the world is caving in around them, and they are in danger of losing their way, we speak truth to dispel the lies.

- Affirmation is about patience. Affirmation waits for the right time, and the right opportunity, and the right words and the right moment – and this may take weeks or sometimes longer.

Ruth and I have attempted to embrace our children's humanness with all the complexities. We have affirmed them as children of God and seen them off on their life-long pilgrimages as Christ's disciples. Practicing affirmation has helped us as a family and as individuals to give up a performance-based lifestyle, with its answer-driven theology, and replace it instead with a *journey* paradigm and theology.

Blessings,

Terry+

Trevor Walters

Appendix 4

Some Healing Centers

UNITED STATES

Christian Healing Center   The Rev. Tim Laundrie
791 Valley Crest Drive
Vista, CA 92084
(760) 295-4266
christianhealingcenter.net

FreshWind Ministries   The Rev. Mike Flynn
4406 Corazon Court
Camarillo, CA 93012
(805) 383-1269
mikeflynn40@gmail.com

Standing Stone Ministry   Jim Hogan
270 Baker Street East, #100
Costa Mesa, CA 92626
(970) 264-9329
standingstoneministry.org

CANADA

Oasis Retreats   Bob Armstrong
Abbotsford, BC, Canada
(604) 832-6792
bob@oasisretreatscanada.com

King's Old Retreat
& Renewal Centre
72049 Hwy 40, North
Cochrane AB
(403) 932 3174

Ellel Canada Ontario
183 Hanna Road RR#2
Westport, Ontario, KOG 1XO
(613) 273-8701
info.calgary@ellelministries.org

Ellel Canada West
#31066 Range Road 20
Didsbury, Alberta, T0M 0W0
(403) 375-4900
info.calgary@ellelministries.org